How to Get a Better Job

Other Titles in the Better Business Series.

How to Start and Run Your Own Business, 7th edition 1989,
M. Mogano

How to Start and Run Your Own Shop, 2nd edition 1988, P. Levene

How to Give a Successful Presentation, 1988, I. Richards

The Shopkeeper's Handbook, 1989, P. Levene

The cover was sponsored by Atlas Employment Agency Limited,
a division of Hestair PLC.

Better Business Series

How to Get
a Better
Job

Mike Mogano

Graham & Trotman

A member of the Kluwer Academic Publishers Group
LONDON/DORDRECHT/BOSTON

Published in 1989 by

Graham & Trotman Limited   Graham & Trotman Inc.
Sterling House   Kluwer Academic Publishers Group
66 Wilton Road   101 Philip Drive
London SW1V 1DE   Assinippi Park
UK   Norwell, MA 02061
                                  USA

© M. Mogano, 1989

British Library Cataloguing in Publication Data

Mogano, M. (Mike)
    How to get a better job.
    1. Job-hunting. Manuals
    I. Title   II. Series
    650.1'4

    ISBN 1 85333 190 2
    ISBN 1 85333 191 0
    ISBN 1 85333 088 4 (Series)

Library of Congress Cataloging in Publication Data

Mogano, M. (Mike)
    How to get a better job / Mike Mogano.
        p.   cm. —— (Better business series)
    Bibliography: p.
    Includes index.
    ISBN 1-85333-190-2 : £14.00 (est.). —— ISBN 1-85333-191-0
    (pbk.) : £6.95 (est.)
        1. Vocational guidance.   2. Career changes.   I. Title.
    II. Series.
    HF5381.M567   1989
    650.14—dc20   89-11949
                                                   CIP

Typeset in Garamond by Colset Private Ltd, Singapore
Printed and bound in Great Britain by
Billing & Sons Ltd, Worcester

Contents

Preface

Improving one's lifestyle is the wish of everyone.

We live in a consumer's world where yesterday's luxuries become today's 'necessities' and where income is king. Available to us is a limitless range of goods and services where our choice is dependent only upon financial capability.

At the same time we desire a way of life which is both meaningful and capable of satisfying our mental abilities.

Achievement of these twin objectives can be secured by improving your career pattern. And that generally means first getting a better job, whether within your present organisation or in pastures new.

In this book I hope I have set out for you, in a structured way, how to go about improving your lot. If you are determined, I have no doubt you will succeed.

I wish you the best of luck!

Please note that throughout this book the use of the male terms 'he', 'him', and so on are used purely for consistency and should always be construed to include equally the female version, for, in employment outlook, never has there been a better time for women to prove that whatever a man can do they can do better!

Mike Mogano

Solihull
July 1989

To Stephen, Nicola, Louise and Michelle — for not getting in the way

CHAPTER 1

What is a Better Job?

So you want a better way of life?

I know that is not what the title says but our lives revolve so much around what we do for a living that we cannot consider one without the other.

It is likely that up to 46 or 48 weeks of the year you will be working. In each of those weeks you will probably be working for five, or even six days. In each day you will be working for, on average, seven or eight hours, sometimes far more. That makes a grand total of approximately 2,000 hours every year. The only other activity likely to demand more of your time is sleep!

Eating, on average, may take up some 700 or so of your waking hours. Sporting activities, if you are so inclined, may account for perhaps 250, unless you are in training for the next Olympics. Watching television, although popular, will not normally account for anywhere near the number of hours you are likely to spend working.

There is no doubt, therefore, that your *working* life has a significant impact upon your *way* of life. It will, for instance, determine the number of hours which you have freely to yourself. And, by implication, it will set the amount of time you have available to pursue your hobbies, interests or sporting activities which, in turn, will affect the quality of your daily life.

Imagine, for example, an employee in a responsible position who is regularly leaving home at seven in the morning, frequently working through his lunch hour and arriving back home, bleary-eyed, at perhaps seven in the evening. How can he possibly enjoy what little free time remains available to him? By the time he has finished his evening meal, it is almost time to begin the cycle all over again. That is no life for anyone. Throw in demands of a husband or wife, add a couple of children, and the picture is even worse.

Family activities will dwindle away. The bread-winner will become just that, and no more. Life will become very dull.

Work Equals Life

The quality of our lives, therefore, is determined almost exclusively by our working environment. Improve one and you improve the other.

A man happy at his work is most likely to be happy at his play. His mind is unlikely to be cluttered with working demands, thus leaving him more free to gain unfettered pleasure from his non-working activities. His life will have more meaning. His family and immediate friends will benefit. And, more likely than not, his mind will be set in a more healthy body.

Is this what you are aiming at? Wanting to get out of your shell and make a real and meaningful life for yourself?

Then changing your job — if you go about it the right way — might just bring about the dramatic change you are seeking. But do not think it will be easy. Certainly not as easy as changing your car. For a start, good jobs are limited; generally speaking, if you are seeking a new car there will be plenty of models awaiting your choice!

And there is the other major difference: with a car, or any other consumer item, it is *your* choice. You may be guided by past experience, a persuasive salesman and certainly by the thickness of your wallet, but, at the end of the day, it is *your* choice.

With a new job, unless you are in the driving seat with a hatful of qualifications and a bundle of experience, it is *someone else's* choice. Your job is to convince him that he has made the right choice.

Convincing the Interviewer

This is not something you achieve simply at the interview. That is merely at the end of a long line of preparation.

First, you will have scanned the market place for an industry or service sector in which you know you can do well. Then you will have pin-pointed a particular company where you believe you can have a future. Finally, in this part of the process, you will have discovered a particular vacancy into which you are convinced you can neatly slot. You will also be able to convince a personnel officer that you are right!

All this will have been followed by some detailed research, a well written curriculum vitae (c.v.) (see Chapter 7), an accompanying convincing letter and the right sort of manner and appearance at the interview itself. The rest is up to you!

Simply to turn up without any preparatory work is to court disaster. Remember, you will not be the only interviewee.

Think of it as war. Each of the other interviewees is your opponent. Each will have his own particular weapon. One may have a scabbard full of qualifications; another could be armoured with a coat of experience. A third may flash a shield of personality.

You cannot, of course, fight them there and then in the waiting room. Each of you will fight your battle alone, in the seclusion of the interview. That is the time your weapons will come into play.

But remember that the sole arbiter of the best weapon is that personnel officer — or perhaps a panel — sitting across the table from you. He has the advantage of having seen each weapon come into play.

Your battle is much harder, for you are fighting in the dark. You will not know whether someone else's sword is sharper than yours or their armour plate shinier.

But if you have prepared for battle as thoroughly as Drake did in the Channel, or Winston Churchill did in Europe, then your chances of scoring a victory will be that much better.

Back to Basics

But you are not in the interview room yet, nor indeed even in the waiting room. The battle has yet to begin.

You are convinced, of course, that you want a *better* job — but are you yet certain that you want a *different* job?

Could your present job be enriched? Are there ways by which, through subtle means, it could *become* a *different* job? Is your employer prepared to listen to suggestions as to how your present position could become a much more meaningful one? Or is he, ostrich-like, so set in the ways of the business that he would treat suggestions from others as derisory, and dismiss them out of hand?

Whatever your views at this stage, this is certainly not an alternative to be ignored. Your boss may yet surprise you!

Have you considered, for instance:

How duties might be arranged more efficiently?
How things might be better organised?
Are opportunities for new business always identified?
Could employee time be more productively used?
Are customers encouraged to come back again?
and so on . . .

Without jeopardizing what you have already, do not be afraid of putting suggestions forward. You may well find an eager employer suddenly sitting up and taking notice of you for the first time. Few employees, particularly in larger organisations, are willing to test the system by suggesting apparently outrageous alternatives to what has already been in existence for some time. Yet, in forward looking organisations, such an employee is welcomed with open arms.

Staff suggestion schemes, of course, exist in most larger companies but these tend to handle matters of detail only, although some of them save the business many thousands of pounds in a year.

We are considering here matters of greater significance: such as who does what, and who is responsible for which areas. In other words, items which help to enrich a job, which can turn a working life of near drudgery into one of lively interest and welcome responsibility.

If you have read to here and put the principles into operation with unexpected success, then I hope that your investment has proved worthwhile.

If all else has failed, however, please read on . . .

What Have You Got Now?

Changing your car, as seen above, is a lot easier than changing your job. The reason, as suggested, is that changing your car is solely your own decision; changing your job involves someone else's.

It is also made easier by the fact that, with a car, you know precisely what you have already. It is either a green, 1985 2-litre model with 23,000 miles on the clock and a few scratches, or, say, a 1981 turbo-charged, without a mark on it and recently boasting a new engine. These are facts which can easily be verified and, apart from looking it over for general condition, a prospective new owner generally knows precisely what he is buying. It may leak a little when he gets it home, but the basic facts remain unaltered.

You might think that such a simple description could equally be applied to your present job. Far from it!

So you thought that you were an office supervisor in the computer industry earning £12,000 per annum? If only a job description were that simple! Let us take a look at it in a little more detail . . .

Sector: Computer software. A relatively new industry, crowded with incomers all eager to share in the apparently unlimited wealth opportunities created by the advent of the computer. Regular corporate casualties as those less efficiently run fall by the wayside.

Company: ABC Limited. Established three years earlier and beginning to find commercial life a little more difficult as others muscle in on its originally specialised field. Working capital resources somewhat tight in view of few fixed assets, yet ongoing research costs high and a long lead time exists between idea and sales.

Your remuneration: Basic £12,000 p.a. Annual bonus has been about £500 and more promised, although will depend upon company's performance. Expenses allowance £30 per month along with a contribution towards mileage worth about £200 a year. Non-contributory pension scheme.

Perquisites (*'perks'*): These could, of course, include a company car (or contribution towards mileage), private health insurance for yourself and/or your immediate dependants, financial assistance towards a mortgage or cheap loans, a share in any profits, subsidised canteen, a discount on company products, help with season tickets, contribution towards telephone costs, sports and social facilities, and, in a few cases, even a day nursery for mothers (or fathers!) with very young children. In your case let us assume that your employer meets the cost of family private health insurance and subsidises, in part, your home telephone bill as it is necessary, on occasions, for you to be available at short notice.

Holiday entitlement: If you are getting more than the 'norm', then this should be taken into account when assessing the total value of your 'package', although it is difficult, of course, to equate it to monetary value. Around 60 per cent of employees in British industry are entitled to 25 days basic leave plus 8 public holidays each year; most of the remainder receive between 30 and 32 days in total, according to the Confederation of British Industry.

All these factors weigh upon your total 'remuneration', even though for some of them you never see any real cash. The payment of private medical treatment by your employer, for instance, may in any one year be worth as 'little' as the premium itself or many thousands of pounds should you, or one of your family, be unfortunate enough to make a claim.

Thus, whilst your basic salary remains at £12,000 p.a., the additional benefits which we have assumed you receive, as stated above, make your financial package worth nearer £14,000. If, in seeking a 'better' job, you are also looking for higher rewards, then this adjustment is something not to be overlooked.

But there are other benefits which you may enjoy and although it may be difficult, or indeed impossible, to convert them into monetary values, they equally must be taken into account when assessing what you have now. They may include:

Performance Related Pay (PRP): Although several chairmen and high-flying executives of major public concerns have for some time seen their pay packet linked to the success, or otherwise, of their company, PRP — following government encouragement — is coming to the masses. As much as 20 per cent of total pay may without penalty be linked to personal performance and several major companies have now introduced a scheme applicable to large sections of their workforce. In the public sector the National Audit Office runs a model scheme based upon eight criteria as follows:

1. Reliability of work.
2. Demonstration of initiative.
3. Demonstration of critical ability.
4. Quantity of work.
5. Planning and organisation of work.
6. Oral communication and relationships.
7. Written communications.
8. Professional skills and management.

This is clearly something to keep your eye on when studying the market for a better job and is expanded upon in Chapter 10.

Job security: Only you can calculate what this is worth to you if indeed it exists! The old 'risk versus reward' ratio applies as much to jobs as it does elsewhere and, quite often, a more poorly paid situation is satisfactory to some for the relative security which goes with it.

Nevertheless, with the major redundancies experienced over the past decade or so, no one can remain entirely safe and job security, therefore, is only as good as your present employer, however efficient and hard working you might be yourself.

Promotion prospects: These will naturally vary widely but, quite clearly, the larger the organisation, then generally the number of opportunities for promotion will be greater. All businesses, great and small, operate within a pyramid shape but the width of those pyramids will differ, as will the policy as to who moves up them with greatest speed. Some — the most progressive — companies will promote upon ability, others tend to adopt a 'dead men's shoes' syndrome, whilst a third group will bring in outsiders to fill more senior posts. From your own experience, you must decide into which category your present employer fits: if you feel you have the ability to carry out greater responsibility but sense that others may be favoured, then certainly you should be seeking a 'better' job, as indeed you are!

Status: This is more important to some people than others. Job titles convey an immediate 'message' in conversation, as the young banker who was actually promoted, after a stint in America as 'Vice President' of a small subsidiary there, to 'Assistant Manager' of a branch back in the UK, quickly found out! American companies, in particular, find they can attract higher calibre candidates for posts enobled with far grander descriptions than we would generally attach here. Again, this is a very personal consideration but do not be fooled by fancy job titles, a subject expanded upon in Chapter 7. A 'Senior Promotions Executive' may be no more than a door-to-door salesman.

Responsibility: This will not add up to much when calculating your present financial worth, but it remains a vital component in any job content to someone, like you, seeking higher pastures. Take one step back, therefore, and list those areas for which you are currently responsible; it may surprise you! Later on (in Chapter 8) you will make use of this list when compiling your c.v.

All these, then, plus a few more attributes, add up to what you have got now.

Do not overlook, also, just how satisfying, or otherwise, the present job is. Does it contain challenges, or is everything put neatly on a plate for you, with little or no opportunity for you to contribute yourself? What level of demand does it make upon you? Is it interesting, or is every day a bore? Does it contain variety, or do you know precisely what you will be doing from minute to minute?

Perhaps most important of all, is it a job requiring only your reaction, or are you allowed — or even encouraged — to initiate ideas yourself?

Add these factors, in as clear a manner as you are able, to the financial figures which were considered earlier and you should have a much clearer picture of where you currently stand in the job market. The task now is to improve that position.

Taking the Decision

You are already part of the way there, through seeking advice. But nothing other than unwavering commitment will do if you are to succeed; there is no half-way house. This book will take you through the necessary stages prior to that firm commitment.

First, you must take full stock of yourself, for unless you know the real 'you', you will not know what you have to sell, because — make no mistake about it — you are about to embark upon a full-blown selling exercise. The prospective buyers — those personnel officers about to take decisions on *your* future career — will be looking your wares up and down and may well be persuaded to buy elsewhere.

So you must be absolutely certain of what you are selling. And, equally importantly, open your stall at the right time. There will be good and bad times to put yourself on the job market.

Above all, a reasoned and structured approach will be essential. Competition, remember, will be fierce, and unfair, and, just as in battle the better prepared soldier's chances of winning are higher, so will yours be if you have planned thoroughly in advance.

This may demand a period of retraining and rethinking and whilst this may at the time prove frustrating, in the long run it will be to your benefit. Opportunities for retraining have never been better and several of these are outlined in Chapter 5.

We will move on to a guide as to where to start looking for your next job move. Available advice is plentiful but you will need to be selective to obtain the most mileage from it.

Then there's a period of writing, writing, writing; initially your own c.v. but thereafter probably dozens of letters in response to job advertisements. Again, selectivity is the key to keep your postage bills manageable.

Handling yourself at the interview will be looked at in some depth, for this is the time when your wares are visibly on display. Who buys when the merchandise does not look good?

In your structured approach to the problem, two avenues of possibility will include working for yourself and spending a period overseas; both will be looked at to enable you either to discard or contemplate one or other of these choices.

Finally, there is a chapter especially for those unfortunate to be disabled, for clearly any handicap only compounds the problem and must be tackled in an equally practical manner.

After the Decision

Hopefully, a cloud will lift once your mind is made up. Tossing and turning around the possibility that you might seek another career is particularly stressful; medical opinion puts it in the category of getting married or a near relative dying, so it is obviously not to be taken lightly.

The deciding process may take several months, during which time you are unlikely to feel your normal self. Your mind will be preoccupied and almost certainly this will have an impact upon those immediately around you.

Because of the nature of your decision-making, it is highly unlikely you will feel able to discuss matters with colleagues at work and the brunt will therefore pass to close relatives and/or friends.

It is important, however, that you seek advice from these sources, as we will see later. The old adage that several heads are better than one was never more true.

Patience and a peace of mind will be required throughout this period, for you will find that a new inner strength is needed to guide you along the right path. Good health will become all important to fund the extra avenues of energy demanded by your new task.

But remember you are not alone. Up and down the country men and women will be struggling with similar decision-making. Your job is to ensure that, for *you*, the right decision has been reached.

So let us now take a good look at YOU . . .

CHAPTER 2

Taking Stock of Yourself

This is quite possibly the most difficult exercise you have ever undertaken. Most of us live two almost entirely different lives. The first is our public, or external, life, the one seen by others, be they friends, workmates or relations, although the closer the relation the more likely that person will see as well our inner, or private, life.

This is the life you now have to reveal to yourself. Paradoxical as it may appear, your inner life is likely to be as closed a book to yourself as it is to others. You are aware of it, of course. You know your inner feelings, your fears, your expectations, your desires better than anyone else. But what you are unlikely to have done before is to lay all these feelings bare, to compile them, to analyse them and to calculate, in a cold, dispassionate manner, just what sort of individual you really are.

It takes guts, and an impeccable sense of honesty. If there is one person in this wide world whom you cannot possibly deceive, it is yourself.

You might, of course, try. You might pep up your true experiences, exaggerate your depth of knowledge, or take a limitless view of your ambitions. But who are you kidding? No one other than yourself and, at the end of the day, you shall be caught out. Maybe not at the interview, maybe not even in the first few months of a new job but, somewhere along the line and invariably at a most crucial point in your intended career, truth will out and the exercise will have proved both fruitless and damaging.

So the first criterion is absolute honesty. The second is objectivity.

Try and take the standpoint of an independent interviewer. Imagine he is someone who actually knows you every bit as well as you know yourself — your inner self, that is, not the exterior facia which you present to the world. Not, for instance, the courageous daredevil unhesitatingly leaping up a 12 foot ladder in order to rescue a cat, but the concerned individual, willing to assist but in truth somewhat scared of heights.

The interviewer has a job to do. He has to question every facet of your personality, every experience, every like and dislike. He must probe your inner feelings, your wishes and your ultimate desires. He must question your degree of honesty with yourself. Do you really, for instance, seek a job with hourly challenges, or would a comparatively quieter life match your temperament? Do you seriously expect to achieve the chairman's post?

And are you being truly realistic when you insist that working 50 or more hours every week would not interfere with your lifestyle?

The interviewer must get everything about you down on paper, in a concise, structured manner. He must question it, analyse it and, finally, seek clear solutions to your desires.

In this case, however, *you* are the interviewer. *You* — the external you — are going to seek straightforward, truthful answers of the other *you* — your real, inner self. You may like, however, to have a little assistance with this very difficult task. Assistance from others.

Before making such a significant step as a career change, the more views you can obtain, the clearer the solutions will become. That is where those around you can come to your assistance.

It may be difficult, of course, to seek the views of those with whom you already work; indeed, it is quite likely to be an impossibility in the circumstances. So look to the family, to friends and to close acquaintances, particularly those most sympathetic to your reasons for seeking a job change.

If you have children, of almost whatever age, do not overlook their views, for the younger generation tend to be less inhibited when advising others. Their ability to cut right through the heart of a problem, although hurtful on occasions, may produce the most candid response of all.

Husbands, wives, sweethearts, second cousins and Great Aunt Jemima — seek them all out. Try your views on them, listen carefully to their replies and build them into your own reactions when weighing up and pros and cons. Do not discard any of their answers, however ludicrous on the surface they may seem, for remember they are seeing only the external *you* and will not know the inner *you* in the way that you do.

So what, more precisely, should we be looking at?

General Principles

First, you should be looking at precisely what you have got now. Unless you are quite certain, you will not be able to judge whether the next job is a better one or not!

So sit down and take a cold, statistical look at your present job. Take full account of any benefits which you currently enjoy which, in your eager search for pastures new, you might otherwise overlook.

What about security? Many jobs once considered relatively secure are no longer in that category and, of course, if you are currently unemployed then this becomes irrelevant. Remember that the longer you have served your present employer, then the more secure you are likely to be — not a golden rule, by any means, but a guideline. So if your present employment stretches back some years think very carefully before changing, for as soon as you begin new employment the more tenuous your position immediately becomes.

However, do not be put off by changing if you are really determined. As we have already seen, you are aiming to change your life as well as your work and however many years you have been in your present post, if you remain disgruntled or dissatisfied, then a carefully planned move is going to do you some good.

Take a look at how many hours you are involved with work; not just the commencing and finishing times, but from the time you leave home in the mornings to when you turn the key again in the evenings. And what about additional work, either in the evening or at weekends?

Weigh up any perks which your job attracts, such as a company car, luncheon vouchers, cheap travel or goods, private medical insurance, and so on. Even a subsidised canteen is worth something. So are your pension rights, if any, and although the law is now making job changes easier as far as these are concerned, they need to be taken into account when assessing what you have got now.

Whatever you have got, however, clearly you are dissatisfied. Now is the time to identify your area or areas of dissatisfaction. Is it:

Your level of remuneration?
Frustration at your level of authority or responsibility?
Working conditions?
Commuting time?
Lack of compatibility with superiors?
Company policy?
Lack of future prospects?

Or indeed, a hundred and one other things, although in practice employee frustration is usually the result of one or more of the above.

You should by now have a list of items — or perhaps just one — of areas causing you to look elsewhere. Keep this by you, for it will help when you come to the process of locating alternative employment. In your search for something better, you will want to ensure that you are not diverted by something superficially attractive but under which may lurk some of the very features you are desperately trying to avoid.

Although in the book title the general word 'job' is used, it is essential that at this stage you define for yourself whether it is a 'job' you are seeking, or a career. We hope to cover both avenues, but they are clearly different, without necessarily clashing. The same job may, for one individual, prove entirely satisfying and stimulating on its own without the need to progress, whilst, for another, it may be seen as a stepping stone only.

Secretarial posts, for example, fulfill both functions. For many secretaries their job is rewarding on its own and they have no particular desire to move away from that function. Others, however, seek to pursue higher roles, perhaps at personal assistant level, or indeed into management itself. Only you can decide whether, for you, a particular job is satisfying and an end in itself, or merely the beginning of a great adventure. Much will depend upon whether or not you have managerial capability and this is the time, also, to establish this point.

Many large companies in the UK firmly believe — although they would probably deny it — that managers are born and not made. Why else would they go to such great lengths to categorise new recruits, either straight from school or from university, into managerial and non-managerial potential? The major banks, for instance, are particularly guilty of such discrimination, thereby often missing out on individuals possessing latent potential unidentified at an early stage and placed in a non-managerial stream.

Potential managers can emerge at any stage and there are hundreds of examples of employees given additional authority and responsibility through extraneous circumstances who subsequently excel themselves and more than justify their unexpected promotion. The lesson is never accept that you are at the peak of your career merely because others say so; if you believe you can achieve more, but not in your present job, then it is time for a change.

Managers, or potential managers, nevertheless have certain character-istics and you may like to conduct a personal assessment. Binder Hamlyn Management Consultants define a manager as an employee who has:

Accountability for the quantity, quality, timing and cost of a particular output of work which is greater than he can perform personally; he therefore has subordinates to whom he can delegate part of the work; and

Authority over his subordinates (within the constraints of the policies of the organisation) to:

veto appointments;
assign work;
assess relative performance;
remove from their roles those whose work does not meet agreed standards.

Not all 'managers', as defined by their own organisation, will possess all of these responsibilities, but the definition does provide an outline of a manager's role. Are you fulfilling it? Or could you do so? Only you can decide.

The Quality of Life

We have already seen the inevitable link between work and life in general and, before you go new job seeking, you must establish how much you are prepared to allow one to impinge upon the other.

There are clearly two extremes. At one end is the 'nine to fiver', unprepared to allow work in any way to interfere with the sanctity of leisure time; at the other, the 'workaholic'. This is someone who enjoys work above all else, invariably to the exclusion of family commitments and is to be avoided at all costs. So too, however, is the former and in reading this far, you are clearly not in that category.

Today's working pressures are such that the 'nine to fiver' will never get beyond that. Go-ahead employers are seeking more commitment now from their employees than ever before and it is only those prepared to give that little extra who will remain in line for promotion. So now is the time to decide:

How many hours am I prepared to commit each day, each week? Will occasional (or even frequent) evening and/or weekend working be tolerated?

What about commuting times? Is another hour or two tacked on each day going to be acceptable? To me? To my family?

Will staying away at night present a problem? Or working overseas for short spells?

How important is the working environment?

How much pressure can I cope with? Does added responsibility act as an adrenalin or does it present problems associated with stress?

Am I prepared to spend additional time on study? What impact could this have on family life?

Do I seek a minimum earnings level? And are certain 'perks' — such as a company car — essential?

Answers to these will provide you with a guide as to the quality of life you are seeking. They are basic questions and must not be ignored at this important stage of your quest. Nor must you attempt to fool yourself with any of the answers. If you know that working unusually long hours will impact adversely upon your health, or family life, then it is pointless looking at jobs in this category.

Now is the time also to take a close look at the things you value most. What follows is not a comprehensive list but covers most people's wishes and, whilst you are ticking yours, it should bring to mind any other particular personal desires you may have:

To be my own boss;
To work alone;
To work with others;
To care for others;
To motivate people;

To be famous;
To help society;
To amass wealth;
To have wide responsibility;
To be creative;
To become expert in something;
To learn new skills;
To operate as a risk taker;
To be competitive;
To have variety;
To lead an active family life.

When you have found those expectations which most closely match yours, list them on a separate piece of paper. These will then become your 'boundaries' when seeking new employment and should prevent you going off at a tangent by the thought of something more tempting yet not meeting your basic criteria.

What you have not ticked form as much a part of your wishes as those you have positively identified with yourself, and these, therefore, should appear below your first list, under the heading 'Negatives'.

Let us assume you have not ticked 'To operate as a risk taker'. This will then exclude you from such occupations as banking or working for yourself. If 'To have wide responsibility' has appeared in your first list, jobs which involve you working mostly on your own will soon become frustrating.

When you reach Chapter 4, have these lists handy for they will form part of your strategic approach to make certain that you are heading in the right direction. Before proceeding any further though, let us examine your own personality.

What Sort of Person Am I?

This is where the honesty really comes in!

Clearly, it is no good whatsoever trying to fool yourself at this stage of your assessment. So try the 'interview' technique suggested earlier. Sit yourself down, imagine there is someone sitting opposite you, and only honest answers count!

Take a look, firstly, at your basic aptitudes, for these will help to tell you in what category you begin to fit. Try the following headings:

Practical: Are you the sort of person who approaches a task in a practical manner, eager to work at it until the solution appears? Do you grab pencil and paper — or spanner and wrench — at the first opportunity when a problem presents itself?

Creative: Do you prefer the artistic approach rather than the practical? Is your solution to problems based more upon ideas, however outlandish they may seem at the time? Are you always trying to change things?

Organised: Do you know where everything is? Are you methodical in your everyday life, returning items to where they 'belong'? Do you insist that your working environment is constantly neat and tidy, where everything has a place? Do you maintain a careful diary of events?

People: Do you motivate others easily? Are you happy in the company of others when working? Does delegation come easily? Do people take notice of your views and can you influence them in times of need? Do you find yourself caring for other people? Are you a natural mixer or a loner?

Verbal: Do you express your thoughts and ideas in a clear and concise manner? Do written reports come over in the same way? Are you at ease in negotiating and communicating your views to others? Do you welcome a strong sense of autonomy?

Numeric: Do figures fascinate you? Do you utilise them to the full when promoting your arguments, either verbally or in reports? Do you use a calculator or computer spread-sheet regularly?

Straight answers to each of these questions will help to 'categorise' you — for we all fall into basic categories when it comes to our natural or acquired aptitudes. Add to your own 'interview report', therefore, the areas as defined above where you score heavily. Equally, if your reaction to any one set of questions is decidedly in the negative, then make a note of this also. If your response is mediocre, then, for the time being at least, ignore that particular aptitude.

Other questions should spring to mind when working through this exercise and, if your answer is a positive 'yes' or 'no', add the item to your list. These might include, for instance:

Am I the sort of person who needs to derive a strong sense of satisfaction from what I do at work?

Is independence essential, or am I prepared to conform?

Do challenges make my day, or do I prefer to be without them?

Am I sensitive to the feelings and views of others, or does the need to achieve targets override such emotions?

Do I dislike working with paper? Does a requirement to record facts and figures excite or appal?

How important is dress to me at work? Am I happier — and more effective — in casual clothes?

Do I have an accent that will impact upon my job?

By now, you should know your real self a little better. And the more honest you have been with your 'interviewer', the more likely you will begin to search for your new career in the right area.

Now take another fresh sheet of paper and let us take a look at:

Your Experience, Skills and Knowledge

Do not dismiss any of these. Wherever you are in life at the present moment, your unlimited brain cells will have accumulated a degree of all three. What you have to do now is to unlock those cells, gather together the information and use it to your greatest advantage.

Take experience first. From the moment our brain starts passing messages to us which we are able sensibly to analyse, we begin to build up a portfolio of experience. Experience in differing food tastes, in places and in our likes and dislikes.

List, therefore, *all* your experiences, however minimal. One week working on an archaeological dig, for instance, will certainly count. So will a holiday abroad, unless the whole time was spent on the beach! Efficiency gained in the Scout or Guide movements will certainly prove useful and so will such diverse 'occupations' as caring for an elderly relative or providing input at a seminar.

Certainly your career pattern to date should be listed, noting details of all functions for which you have been responsible and experience gained along the way.

List each job held. Describe its requirements and the experience it called for. Note your starting and finishing dates and, importantly, just why you left. If you received promotion, consider why it was earned.

Job descriptions are essential here, as opposed merely to job titles. 'Assistant buyer', for instance, will not help you to fill in your experience league table; rather, it should read: 'assistant buyer, responsible for purchasing raw materials (special steels, fasteners, welding equipment, sundries) up to values of £250,000 for prefabricating in water treatment industry; negotiating prices and delivery times; maintaining supplier records; telephonic and personal contact with suppliers; discussing technical needs with draughtsmen, engineers; assisting with measurements of quantities, etc.'

What did you achieve during this period? Were savings made, or budgets met? Were you responsible for introducing cost-saving measures, streamlining systems or changing traditional buying methods? With what new products or processes were you involved during this time?

Do not miss anything. Depending upon your age, your sheet of paper headed 'Experience' should have plenty recorded upon it — certainly one full sheet for every five working years, although you may care to reduce the number of pages where, for instance, you have worked in only one or two positions for some lengthy time.

Hopefully by now you will also have developed certain significant 'skills', although at first you may need to clear your mind a little in order to identify these. We all add skills to our personal portfolios, but may not immediately recognise them.

Do you, for instance, drive a car? Then there is one, hopefully, immediately. Can you drive a hard bargain? Then add 'negotiating' to your list. Are you generally patient and persuasive when transferring knowledge to others? If so, then you will be skilful in teaching.

By now you should have got the idea. To prompt you into further additions to your list, do you fit into any of the following categories:

Advising others.
Managing people.
Motivating colleagues.
Meeting people's needs.
Analysing.
Recording.
Researching.
Creating.
Making.

Your list should, by now, be looking a little more full than you perhaps anticipated when you started this session. Finally, let us take a look at 'knowledge'.

This attribute should not be confused with the first two, experience and skills. Your experience might include, for instance, some time spent in an advisory capacity to a superior during which time your skills in, say, negotiating became more finely tuned. At the same time, however, you will have added to your storehouse of knowledge in whatever subject you were dealing with. Thus you will have benefited in all three areas during this aspect of your working life.

Knowledge is clearly a function of the mind. The capacity of our brain is limitless and — whilst remembering it may be a different matter altogether — we are thus able to store vast amounts of information, ready to be called up at a second's notice. Providing your store is above average in any particular subject, then clearly you have the benefit of knowledge over and above others. That advantage must be put to effective use in the job market.

So add to your list any areas, however diverse, in which you believe your knowledge is a little better than that of the average man. Again, do not miss anything, whether it relates to vocational areas or otherwise; we are still trying to identify the real *you*.

Interests, Talents, Hobbies

Naturally, any leisure pursuits will provide a clue as to what really interests you.

How we all envy the golf professional, being paid on a regular basis for something which he really loves doing. Or the jockey who lives for horses. Perhaps even the steeplejack whose greatest ambition is to get away from it all!

The reality may be very different, but if it is possible to combine one's working life with a positive leisure interest, a heightened degree of satisfaction is likely to be the result. The opportunity will remain for the privileged few but now is the time at least to identify those pursuits you would gladly follow for no pay at all!

Are you a music lover, a fisherman, or an avid reader? Do you like turning wood, hill walking or collecting butterflies? Does writing poetry turn you on? Whatever your 'sideline', make a written note of it, along with any specialised aspects which particularly interest you.

When it comes to a structured job search, your personal interests will be made use of as far as this is possible.

Qualifications

Start at the beginning and work from there. Initially, therefore, take schooling and a full list would include some of the following:

> Ordinary and Advanced Levels GCE (or GCSE)
> Degree
> Post Graduate Degree
> Doctor of Philosophy
> City and Guilds qualifications
> RSA qualifications
> TEC and BEC qualifications
> Membership of professional bodies
> MBA
> etc.

Include any specialised courses attended, as well as participation in conferences, seminars and so on. Do not overlook correspondence courses and, indeed, even any weekend instructional sessions.

Special projects undertaken at work can be included in this list for, as you will see later, it will guide you along certain avenues which you might otherwise not have contemplated.

You may perhaps be a little thin in this area. Do not despair. In Chapter 5 we will be taking a close look at how you can — given time — add to your qualifications to make you more attractive in the job market.

Limitations

There is, of course, little advantage to be gained in viewing the entire spectrum of the market place if you feel the need to limit your horizons in any way. So now is the time to be perfectly straightforward with yourself again in clarifying any limitations which you will be setting yourself.

There is little point in adding 'fully mobile' to your c.v. if you — or your spouse and children — are not going to be at all happy in relocating your home several hundred miles away. Equally, if job security is of vital importance to your plans, joining a small new venture in unknown territory is hardly likely to make you feel comfortable.

There are four major areas in which you might wish to set yourself clear boundary lines:

Financial

Here you have to be realistic both about your true commitment level and your ambitions. First, define your present level of expenditure and adjust it for any items you know are truly 'luxuries' — at least, in your view. Luxuries, of course, are subjective and one man's weekly expenditure of £40, say, on entertaining may in his eyes be essential to the business he is in, whilst to an onlooker it may appear ridiculously extravagant. Similarly, some of us will think nothing of spending, say, £50 on a pair of shoes but hesitate at paying much more than £25 for a meal for two, whilst our neighbour may eat for double the cost but buy his shoes on the market.

Which item is the luxury? Ask 10 people and you will get them arguing all night!

In any event, we all tend to spend most of what we earn, hopefully after putting a little by for a rainy day. It is rather like buying a new coffee table — within a day or so, its surface is, at least in part, filled. How did we manage without the additional surface beforehand? Given a rise, we will look around for ways of spending it!

So take a hard look at what your present earnings go on; if there is a little fat about, cut it out. That will give you an indication of your minimum 'subsistence' level. Convert this figure into something a little higher — for we must all aim at the stars — and you will have arrived at your starting point. Make the necessary adjustments, as explained in the previous chapter, for 'perks' of any kind, and you have something positive to use as a baseline.

Family

Perhaps, at heart, the most serious consideration of all. If you are part of a family, as suggested earlier, then work will be part of your life — your family life.

If your partner is working also, it may have to be a 'partnership' of working hours for, if there are children to be taken into the formula, sufficient free overlap time will be needed if the family is to function normally.

Two parental bread-winners is far from uncommon today and a lot of serious thought should go into your decision on a career change if harmony is to remain. What does your partner think about your choices? Do not, whatever else you do, ignore their views and, if the children are old enough to offer meaningful advice, listen to them also. Keep an open mind and be wary of dismissing family opinions — you are still going to have to live with each other after the deed is done!

Social and sporting interests should also be considered here. If the demands of a new, hopefully higher level job could curtail any such activities, are you prepared to put up with a different life style? Is your family? Just how important are the children's tennis lessons, or your social club life?

Children's education will not, I am sure, be overlooked. Whether this is private or state provided, if a change appears necessary, attention to it should appear high on your priority list. New schools need investigating, head teachers should be quizzed, curricula studied and transportation methods discovered.

Mobility

Do you really want to move is the basic question you must ask yourself, and your family, at this point.

Although some 185,000 families sell up and move to a different area every year to enable at least one member to take up a new appointment, it remains without doubt a most unnerving experience. Neither a flat nor a buoyant market helps because, in the former, your house sale may take months to complete, whilst if everything is moving rapidly, prices tend to follow suit and you cannot afford to be out of the market for even a short length of time.

Not only the cost, but the hassle, therefore, of moving house must be fully considered. If your new employer is to pay all, or even a proportion of, removal expenses, then this will help to relieve the anxiety, although the problem of selling, and finding a replacement home, will remain. Fortunately, many specialist relocation companies now exist, although they tend to act on behalf of employers as opposed to offering their extremely useful services to individuals and you should, therefore, enquire of your potential new employer whether or not this facility is available. We will take a closer look at this when considering how interviews should be tackled, later in the book.

A small firm which offers individuals advice on moving home is National Starpoint based at Alexandra House, Sandon Road, Stafford and run by Jeremy and Jennifer Eadie who set up in business when their own house move fell through and they realised that there had to be hundreds of families in similar, often desparate, situations.

National Starpoint will sort out everything connected with a move for you, from advising regional house prices to the telephone number and surgery opening hours of the nearest doctor, which can prove to be important to someone with a young family. They have produced thousands of 'local guides' which cover everything from the time it will take you to get to work, with a whole range of alternative routes, to the membership fees of the local golf club, the pick of the area's restaurants, theatres, and even the architectural flavour of the nearest towns. Picture postcards accompany the guides.

Moving could radically alter your lifestyle. But, unless you investigate fully the pros and cons beforehand, the alteration may not be to your liking.

Commuting habits, in particular, differ widely around the country. Whilst it may be possible in country districts to reach your place of work in less than half an hour, and even occasionally return home for lunch, such luxuries are not generally available to those commuters in the densely populated suburban areas where up to three hours travelling time daily is far from unusual. It may be possible, of course, to use this time effectively from a working standpoint, and files, dictation machines and even portable telephones are commonly seen features on the south easterly rail network.

But is this for you? Is a working day which starts at perhaps 6 a.m. and finishes at 7 p.m. acceptable, bearing in mind the inevitable adverse impact upon family and social life?

Only you, and your family, can decide. But do not dither. It is imperative that you make up your mind at this stage whether or not you are truly mobile. If you are, then your job search can be suitably widened; if not, then decide upon an acceptable catchment area in which to look.

Security

This factor is not always given the consideration it deserves. Some people are born entrepreneurs, ready to risk all and take a gamble, and invariably they win. Others opt for the safer life. Instances are legion and can be detected from secondary school onwards. Remember the boy who had the most marbles and who was always ready to exchange, for a price? Or the university student who regularly had something to sell, and who seemed to have a higher lifestyle than everyone else?

In adult life, entrepreneurs stick out like suntanned bodies on a British beach. By nature — but not always — self-employed, their assets are ever changing, their more casual approach to life noticeable. Which category are you in? If you hesitate, then almost certainly you fall into the 'more secure' category!

There is nothing to be ashamed of here. If a 'secure' job accompanied by satisfactory working conditions and, eventually, an acceptable pension all fall within your horizons, you need take note only and build these factors into your strategy when overseeing the job market. Self-employment opportunities need not be scanned, nor 'high-flying' jobs calling for risk takers, thus saving yourself valuable time in identifying that 'better job'.

Before taking the next step, a priority list is going to prove invaluable.

Priorities

By now, you should know yourself a little better. You will, hopefully, have taken stock of your present situation, and highlighted those areas which, for you, now present special opportunities.

Look back upon what you have recorded and pluck out those points which seemed most relevant at the time. Perhaps particular personality features were instantly recognisable, or you suddenly realised that knowledge you had acquired in the past could now be put to practical use. Whatever impacted upon you most forcefully is likely to play a vital part in your job search and should at this stage be written down again.

You might now have three or four brief points which will become your priorities. On some aspects you may need to compromise. Ideally, an out of door occupation may have attracted but, on reconsideration, one allowing you possibly 70 per cent of the time in the fresh air may be acceptable. Income levels, or commuting times, might require some fresh thought to provide wider 'consideration bands', broadening the scope of your search.

You should also, by now, know your own strengths and weaknesses. The strengths you must clearly play on. If necessary, elaborate them within tolerant acceptability, bearing in mind that they must stand up to questioning later. But do not ignore them; they may be an important card in your winning hand.

Weaknesses identified should be dealt with as circumstances demand. Frequently, they may be ignored but, if more prominent, they may need to be eliminated. Chapter 5 will take care of this for you.

CHAPTER 3

Timing Your Departure Sensibly

Inevitably, there is a good time to leave a job and a bad time. If you are in a position to control this timing, then paying some attention to it will further enhance your opportunities as you enter your new state. If, of course, you are already unemployed, then this becomes academic, although later on we will take a look at how at least you can help keep body and soul together during this trying time.

Perhaps the first exercise is to quiz yourself once again as to just why you are even considering other opportunities. Ask yourself the following questions:

How long have I worked in this particular sector, and would my career gain by switching to something different?

How long have I worked for this particular company and would my c.v. benefit from further experience elsewhere?

Have I spent too much time in this particular job, and could I be getting out of touch with other areas of experience?

Am I in a set career pattern — or a dead-end job?

What does the future hold for my particular employers? Do they keep pace with the times?

Am I losing out in my salary scale?

Clearly, the answers will help you to confirm or deny the need for a switch at this stage of your career. What you are seeking to do, if you are truly ambitious, is to strengthen and deepen your own c.v. to the point that eventually you are ahead of the field. And, remember, the field is a very big one.

The time of year when you should be making the big switch is probably irrelevant unless you are operating in an industry, such as construction, which itself is influenced by other than man-made factors. Even here, however, and certainly at management level, this is not of overriding importance. If the possibility of working abroad is included within your horizons (and later a special chapter is devoted to this), then seasonal fluctuations may just possibly have to be considered. All in all, however, weather will play only a minor part, whilst your own degree of preparation will feature far more prominently.

Holidays — if you feel you should be thinking about them at all — may need careful planning. It would be foolish, for instance, to have begun your careful forethought and begin to make moves towards seeking something better and then disappear from the scene during what might prove to be a crucial time. You will certainly not welcome a note pushed through your front door, on your return, from a prospective new employer to say that he had been disappointed in not making contact but had regrettably since filled the post!

Look Around You

Do be aware at all times of any changes which are taking place in your present organisation. Keep your ears very close to the ground and make certain you are well informed so that, should your own job become vulnerable, you will have a decent interval to complete your strategic planning.

Take-overs, of course, happen overnight not infrequently and, if this were to occur and you felt your job threatened, then little immediate evasive action would be possible. Reading your own trade press, however, and listening to as much informed 'gossip' as possible may just forewarn you of a potential predator's interest.

Equally, the likelihood of a merger will probably be known to a selected few only, although your own discreet information gathering may put you ahead of some of your colleagues if an overlap in jobs points to possible redundancies. If you can be ahead of the pack when heads begin to roll, your chances of gaining something a little superior to your peers elsewhere will prove your reward.

Might your section or division be in danger of closing, or amalgamating with another, resulting in a lower overall head count? Signs of this often clearly abound, although the more timid may prefer to bury their heads in the sand. It may well be, of course, that it is another division which is coming to the end of its useful life, but yours may act in a support capacity and thus itself be just as vulnerable.

Have you noticed any marked change in policies within the organisation lately? Ones which could indicate a change in direction, or be an attempt to avert basic problems such as profitability or return on capital? Seek information from those most likely to be in possession of it, rather than from the rumour mongers who exist in every workplace, to allow you to gauge the effect upon your own position.

If senior personnel appear to be changing at a regular rate this will almost certainly mask corporate difficulties, not necessarily evident to in-line employees. Again, ask questions and, indeed, you may well find your inquisitiveness paying dividends in the evident longer-term interest you are showing in your company. If senior employees appear to be following contrasting objectives, there is no reason at all why you should not come to your own decision as to the most sensible direction and attach yourself to those following that policy, for as day follows night all of those senior executives will not survive. If you find yourself having backed a 'loser' in these circumstances, put it down to experience!

Changes in an organisation may, of course, impact upon your own situation in a far more personal way, although subtle changes need more careful assessment if you are to prepare yourself for a potential job loss.

If some of your supervisory functions are removed, in a manner not fully explained, then clearly someone has changes in mind. Perhaps you have been taken off your normal duties completely, and whilst the suggestion may be that this is temporary — and indeed you may find the alternatives stimulating for a while — some deeper reasoning may well lay behind the decision.

If others approximately on your own level appear to be enjoying a greater degree of managerial confidence than you are, you must ask yourself why. If, additionally, decisions traditionally in your sphere are being taken elsewhere, or perhaps being questioned or delayed, again some investigation for the real reasons is called for on your part.

Be fully aware, therefore, at all times of the interaction between your own responsibilities and the needs of the organisation for which you work. As long as the two mutually coincide then all is probably well. As soon as cracks begin to appear in what was once a smooth interface, the time for questioning begins.

The first question must be: 'Is my job still safe?' and the second: 'Should I be planning a move?' If the answer to the latter is in the affirmative, the key word is 'planning', and timing will play a vital part in that plan.

You should avoid, at all costs, leaving under a cloud. Almost certainly any prospective employer will be making his searches upon you and the more kindly disposed your present employers are to your leaving, the more favourable their response is likely to be.

Do not, therefore, walk out in a huff. Grasp the opportunity to explain both to your superiors and to any colleagues working directly under you your reasons for leaving — which, in the circumstances, may demand a little artistic licence! Leave, however, as a friend and not as an enemy for this will benefit no one, least of all yourself.

Do some homework first on your legal position and make certain that you give the required period of notice in the terms of any contract which exists. Generally, if no such contract has been signed, then the period of notice which you will have to provide normally equates with your pay intervals.

Do not be too rash to leave, however, if you have yet to find yourself an alternative job. It is an accepted — and proven — fact that your chances remain better if you are currently employed. But what if you have no choice?

Being Asked to Leave

This could take several forms, as follows:

Bankruptcy or insolvency of your employer
Redundancy
Being fired

and we will take a closer look at each in turn.

Bankruptcy

The first of these possibilities is unlikely to come as a complete shock to a thinking employee for there will normally be a few clues in evidence beforehand. Regular customer complaints may prove to be a sign, as will be a diminishing order book, deliveries of limited supplies, laying-off of staff, and, particularly, any delays in paying of wages. Whilst innumerable reasons exist for a company's demise, the actual end comes as a result of the drying up of cash, ultimately due to employees.

Your immediate course of action is to make contact with the liquidator or receiver who will be appointed, although do not anticipate early payment for it is not unusual for a liquidation to take 6 or 12 months, or even longer, to be finalised. You will receive preferential treatment before any unsecured creditors but, clearly, if the company has no money at all, you could be in for a complete loss.

You may consider it worthwhile consulting your solicitor if you are owed a great deal but, generally, a reputable liquidator or receiver will offer you sound advice.

Redundancy

Tens of thousands of workers in this country have known the harsh face of being made redundant, some of them several times over, especially in hard hit areas. Some, of course, have welcomed it, particularly those nearing retirement age and where exceptionally good redundancy terms have been arranged.

It is important, however, to observe the niceties of the law relating to the subject, in this case the Employment Protection Act. Providing you have been asked to depart due to 'cessation or diminution of work of a particular kind in a particular place', then you should be entitled to employee rights under the Act, including payment based upon your length of service, providing this exceeds two years.

Equally, once you receive your redundancy notice, you may in fact leave straight away providing that both you and your employer agree in writing to this course of action. You will still be entitled to your statutory pay but will have an opportunity of job searching rather than working out your 'notice'.

Being Fired

Although not so prevalent today, some employers have attempted to use redundancy as a front for firing an employee and if you feel this is the case, and that you have been dismissed unfairly, then do take legal advice. Your solicitor, if he is well versed in employment matters, may well advise you to appeal to an industrial tribunal.

Your former employer, on the other hand, may be embarrassed if he feels that he has a weak case and you could be in for substantial compensation without the need to go to law. Similarly, if you win your case at a tribunal, this is likely to prove a fruitful as well as a moral victory although inevitably such appeals take time and you may prefer to get on with the job of finding another, better appointment.

Remember, also, that to lose your case at a tribunal is likely to have just the opposite effect, i.e. moral despair and loss of time and, probably, money. And whether you win or lose, it is just possible that your next potential employer may be somewhat guarded in taking you on for the very fact that you sought legal redress. You cannot change human nature!

Being given notice, for whatever reason, can have side benefits in that employers are often willing to allow an employee to leave immediately and you would, therefore, have a period in which to seek alternative employment whilst at the same time being paid.

Tax benefits can also arise in this situation due to the tax laws which charge normal rates upon earned income but provide allowances upon either redundancy payments or monies paid on an ex gratia basis. There are, however, limits to these reliefs, although the tax treatment is in general quite generous.

Legal advice in these circumstances also is advisable since any payments made to you need to be properly described to qualify for relief. If you have a written employment contract, then particular care is called for.

Industrial Tribunals

What are your chances of success if you elect for this route?

Tribunals of this nature receive over 30,000 complaints every year, most of them relating to unfair dismissal. All of these do not, however, reach the courts themselves and about two-thirds are resolved outside. Of the remaining 10,000 or so, about one-third are found in favour of the employee.

Legal representation is not absolutely necessary, but the complexities of employment law suggest that you are more likely to succeed if an expert is called on your behalf. Your former employer will almost certainly find himself a first-class solicitor and may well track one down who specialises in this area. For you, as a layman, to argue each point as it arises against someone dealing daily with such matters is to ask for trouble unless you are especially persuasive and believe that a lay approach might win the day.

If you do decide to take legal advice, give your expert plenty of time to prepare his case. Courts will not be sympathetic to badly presented appeals.

Cost cannot be ignored and can be substantial. The stronger you feel your case is, the more justified will be the expenditure which, in the event of success on your part, will normally be reimbursed.

Advice can be obtained from the Advisory, Conciliation and Arbitration Service (ACAS) which has a set Code of Practice.

Golden Handshakes

If you are a member of one of the major trade unions, then an agreement probably exists to determine any 'additional' payments to which you might be entitled upon termination of your employment. Managerial and executive personnel, however, tend not to be in this 'privileged' position and therefore need to negotiate their own terminal benefits. This can turn out to be a particularly difficult exercise for someone unused to it, as indeed most of us would be.

It might be useful to know, therefore, that severance payments can certainly extend to 18 months' salary dependent upon length of service, although clearly the events surrounding your departure will have an influence upon the generosity or otherwise of your employer! Any contract which you may have with him may also set out conditions upon departure and could possibly, under the Companies Acts, provide for up to five years' compensation.

Do not think, though, that if you have the benefit of such a contract, you are automatically entitled to payment for the unexpired period, for this is certainly not the case. The courts, if it comes to this, will almost certainly compensate you but for breach of contract only and you will remain responsible for mitigating your circumstances, if appropriate, by finding another job.

A friendly settlement with your employer is by far the best course of action, for a court hearing will be delayed and there is no certainty of your victory. Your age, state of health and likely potential in the job market will all be taken into account — and you may find that a legalistic view of the latter is far different from your own!

If a golden handshake is offered, do not be greedy but do not grasp it immediately either. Give yourself some thinking time and an opportunity to chat it over with your family or professional friends which could temper your initial thoughts, be they magnanimous or resentful.

Any compensation should be based not merely upon your salary level, but any fringe benefits, such as a company car, private health insurance and so on should be taken into account. We have already seen how these 'add-ons' can significantly improve your overall level of remuneration and it is upon this adjusted total that any 'handshake' should be based. Holiday entitlement may also come into any formula which is agreed.

The financial position of your employer will naturally impact upon the level of his generosity and, no doubt, the relationship which you have had with him over the years may also affect his treatment of you. For this reason alone, it remains a wise policy never to seriously fall out with your employer.

Taking Care of the Future

There has recently been a major legislative step forward to benefit people like you, i.e. job changers. This has been in the field of personal pensions where every employee now has the right, if he so wishes, to leave his own company pension scheme and make his own pension arrangements. This will clearly affect your own position now that you are considering changing jobs.

Legally, you will be entitled — providing you have been in your current employer's scheme for at least two years — to a preserved pension. This may not, however, pay out as well as if you had stayed in your present job, for whilst in this case your entire pension would be based upon your final pay at retirement, if you leave earlier then obviously the preserved portion will be based only upon your salary level upon leaving.

Your employer is now bound, by law, to increase that portion of your pension 'bucket' established since January, 1985 by the movement in the Retail Price Index or 5 per cent (whichever is the lower) each year. Many of the better employers will increase the entire preserved pension.

The amount in the bucket is known as the 'transfer value' and you can take this with you, either depositing it with your new employer or, alternatively, setting up your own personal scheme.

The impact upon your post-retirement earnings demands very careful consideration before you commit yourself to a move, although this will probably not be an overriding factor if you are under, say, 40. Between this age and 50 it will need looking at carefully and, over 50, even more so. With the new legislation, however, you are in a better position than you were previously, where some people would, in effect, not be able to afford to move.

If you decide to move your transfer value to your new employer's scheme, he will use this to buy you an annual sum on retirement, to top up his own scheme benefits, or to purchase 'years' in his scheme.

If you see yourself making several job moves during your career you would be well advised to take a serious look at establishing your own, personal scheme. And certainly if you are one of the 10 million employees in this country without any private pension arrangements, then you should start one immediately.

By doing this you can either contract fully out of the Government's own pension scheme — known as SERPS (State Earnings Related Pension Scheme) — or top up your SERPS entitlement. If you have less than 20 years before you retire, then it will probably pay you to stick with SERPS if this is all you have. If you are under, say, 45, though, you can probably better the Government's scheme by looking at personal pensions.

These are of the 'money purchase' variety, i.e. your contributions (and your employer's) are invested and, upon retirement, you use the lump sum — which will have grown with interest — to buy yourself a pension. What you get will depend very much upon the level of contributions and how well the investments fare; there are no guarantees.

You and your employer, incidentally, will still pay the full National Insurance contributions even if you contract out of SERPS, although part will be credited to your plan by the Department of Social Security and, additionally, your scheme will benefit from basic rate tax relief on your own National Insurance contributions.

Remember, when comparing the possibility of setting up your own plan, that there can be more benefits than merely post-retirement pay. Death in service benefits, widows' pensions and so on often form part of an employer's scheme, for he will have greater bargaining power when establishing his scheme than you will have as an individual. It is unlikely that you will obtain anything better than that offered by major employers but, if you see regular job changes for yourself, then a private plan will not be upset by these.

If comparing new schemes, check the following:

What retirement ages are quoted?

Is there a pension for your spouse if you die first?

What allowance, if any, is made for increases in your retirement pay to take account of inflationary movements?

Is there the ability to exchange some of your retirement pay for a cash sum?

Precisely what happens on death in service?

Alternatively, what is the position if you die shortly after you retire?

The Company Pensions Information Centre, at 7 Old Park Lane, London, W1Y 3LJ, (Telephone 01–493–4757), produce first-class brochures on the subject.

Keeping Body and Soul Together

If you are unlucky enough to find yourself in a period of unemployment in between jobs, then you may well qualify for benefit and the Department of Social Security publish leaflets (NI 12 and NI 196) outlining these.

You may feel that your pride will be hurt by claiming such benefits, especially if this is your first experience of being out of a job. All you are really doing, however, is seeking reimbursement of your own National Insurance contributions, possibly representing several years' payments. At the same time, it can actually be to your disadvantage not to register as unemployed and visit a Department of Employment office to prove that you are available for work, since this can affect your rights to state pensions and certain other benefits.

You will not, of course, find it easy to live on unemployment benefit alone and you may find yourself dipping into personal savings, which could seriously affect any budgeting you may have carried out to see you through to the next job; this is looked at in the next chapter.

Whilst you must make yourself available for work, you are not obliged to take anything which a job centre offers you, although clearly you will not be expected to place too many onerous restrictions upon what you are prepared to take. On top of any benefits, it is sometimes possible to obtain assistance towards attending job interviews if they are some distance away.

Unemployment benefit ceases after one year although if you can prove real hardship then a claim for Income Support can be made. Leaflet SB 21 issued by the DSS will help you to assess your position and provide guidance as to whether you are eligible.

Your next task equates with a military exercise, so don your peaked cap, take your Field Marshal's baton out of its rucksack and prepare for action!

CHAPTER 4

Planning a Structured Approach

The way ahead is clear — you want a better job.

That established, you need to know the best way of setting out your stall. You have something to sell and must present your product in the most attractive manner. It will not, of course, be the only product on sale and many others may prove more attractive to the buyer.

You need to go about the exercise, therefore, in a workman-like — indeed, commercial — manner.

Someone establishing himself in the market place to sell shirts, or even tomatoes, would not merely stand on a street corner and set up stall. He would find out details of the competition, establish price levels and costs, look into any legal aspects, hire an accountant, and so on. If you are going to be successful in selling what is the most difficult thing in the world to sell — yourself — your own research must be every bit as thorough.

It may come as something of a shock, but the first hurdle your mind has to clear is the fact that no one actually needs you. If you feel this to be untrue, consider the hypothetical case that you emigrate tomorrow to a deserted island in the middle of the Pacific Ocean. Which employer would actually despatch a liner, imploring you to return?

Having agreed on that point, let us proceed!

You thus have a product to sell which no one really requires. Your attributes may admittedly match a vacant position existing somewhere or other, but equally suitable candidates will be waiting in the wings. Your task is to convince an employer that he actually needs *you*.

Selling yourself, therefore, is little different from selling a can of beans — and do not for one moment think that is simple. Behind every can on the supermarket shelf is a vast publicity department, backed up by experts on every subject from advertising, through design to such fields as accounting, distribution and printing. The difference with selling yourself is that you will not have that array of specialists to assist you, so it will actually be that much harder.

Do not overlook the importance of your task. Treat it casually, and you are likely to finish up with a causal job. But put some real marketing behind your efforts and you will be well rewarded.

One final reminder, before you start setting yourself some objectives. It is generally easier to find a new job if you are already working than if you are not. There is no logical explanation for this but the fact remains that employers generally prefer to take candidates from another organisation than from the unemployed. This is, of course, most unfair but then life never was fair, was it?

Setting Objectives

The first one you have already firmly established — that of finding yourself a new, and better, job. Take a piece of paper and write that in bold letters across the top. Now what else must you clarify in your own mind before you even start looking?

Much will depend on your present age, what level you have reached in your present organisation, current salary and ambition.

This is the time to be practical. A 30 year old on £16,000 per annum is NOT going to step on to a main Board of a major company and double his salary, nepotism, of course, apart. So rule one in setting your objectives is to be realistic and take career progression one step at a time. If an employer is seeking someone 'in mid career, with 10 years' experience', 25 year olds clearly need not apply, although there will always be the odd (very odd) exception where you might cheekily chance your arm if you believe you positively fit the bill.

In general, however, set your sights by all means somewhere beyond your present capabilities but not too far into the blue!

Ask yourself where you would like to be in 10 years time. An indication of industry, position, responsibility and salary expectation (at current rates) will help to pin-point exactly where you see yourself going and you can then begin to fill in possible avenues down which you will need to travel to get there.

Once you have flagged these indicators, jot them down below your heading and use them as guiding stars when you begin your search in earnest. They need not, of course, be set in concrete and you may indeed decide on a change of direction after your initial research. Flexibility is the key at this early stage, but when you feel you have interrogated yourself sufficiently as to your future desires, then obviously it would be unwise to detract too severely from the four main paths you have set yourself: industry, position, responsibility and salary indicator.

Mobility

This is probably the most important potential limiting factor when taking stock of your situation and, particularly, when setting your objectives.

If you, and your family, are quite content to live out your lives in your present abode, or within a set catchment area, there is nothing at all wrong with that — as long as you recognise its effect upon your own long-term capability. On the assumption that you wish to return home each evening, or at least a majority of them, employment will be limited to whatever is available within an acceptable commuting distance.

. Many national and international companies have their headquarters in London and top jobs can often only be reached via the metropolis. Whilst daily commuting to the capital is continually extending outwards, there must come a limit and, if your sights are set high, London will have to be included in them. A spell abroad may also be necessary as a prerequisite to achieving career horizons and all these possibilities need taking into account during your objective setting exercise.

Whatever anyone may argue, the North-South divide really does exist and it would be as well to be acquainted with the facts from a recent Government report.

- Highest average earnings exist in the South East, but so does the highest road accident rate;

- The cheapest homes are in the North, but crime is higher;

- The West Midlands has more people employed in manufacturing than any other area;

- Wales can boast both the lowest road accident rate and lowest crime rate;

- Scotland has the lowest ratio of pupils to teachers;

- East Anglia has the fastest growing population, making jobs that much easier to find;

- The highest rate of unemployment is found in Northern Ireland.

Throw all these factors into a pot and it is not easy to make decisions about mobility, or lack of it. Nevertheless, a decision must be made to help you in your job search and you would be unwise to ignore the point; it will not 'take care of itself'.

Some employers, desperate to lure workers from the North, offer eye-catching 'rewards', including mortgages of up to £75,000 to bridge the house price gap, although these have to be repaid if the new employee leaves his job, along with a proportion of any profit when the new house is sold.

Categories of workers eligible for these schemes, on offer by some London local authorities, include analysts, auditors, building surveyors, accountants, social workers, occupational therapists, solicitors, valuers, trading standards officers and certain craft workers.

Do not let the cost of moving put you off, for this should quickly be 'recouped' either through a higher salary or possibly increasing home values.

The actual cost of a move has gone up very little over recent years due to competition between the professionals involved, in particular solicitors and estate agents.

What Can You Earn?

Money is not, of course, as everyone will tell you, the ultimate criterion. But it does pay the bills.

Although many people will say that they 'enjoy the challenge', 'feel needed', 'like the environment', or even 'would work for nothing', in truth the pay packet at the end of the week or month has to be sufficiently stimulating to keep them there. Most of us ultimately spend the largest slice of what we earn and if we wish to raise our standard of living we must simply earn more.

This is not to ignore our individual views on the quality of life. There are those, by the thousand, who would not for any money work in London or, indeed, anywhere in the bustling South East. For them, the relative peacefulness of, say, Devon or Yorkshire pays quality dividends which could not be matched by mere increases in pay.

A recent 'Reward' cost of living survey found that the same living standards could be maintained in the Midlands and the North on a salary equating to very much less than that paid in London and the South East. So, when looking at pay scales, take into account where you are likely to be based.

The challenge which a new job presents may still influence you of course and, indeed, a study of executive mobility showed that rewards and status came well behind a quest for challenge, the need for recognition, and opportunities to learn more and be creative. Over 2,000 members of the British Institute of Management were questioned and, interestingly, it was also found that managers between the ages of 25 and 40 changed their jobs on average every three years. In three-quarters of the cases, a change of function accompanied a job change.

When setting your salary horizon, be realistic and remember that certain factors will limit your price:

Your age and experience;

Your qualifications;

Whether or not you are currently employed. You might think that this should not affect the matter but, in practice, it regrettably does;

Whether you wish to remain in the same function or not;

And, if you are moving into something entirely different, whether it has a differing salary structure.

If you are not entirely familiar with the market you hope to enter, your research will have to take in regular reading of job advertisements before you will be in a position to set your salary level.

. This should, ideally, be set between two bands. The lower figure will be more appropriate if you are aiming for something relatively new; the higher if you are seeking promotion in a field in which you are already well qualified or experienced, or both.

As we have said before, look beyond the salary scale to any side benefits, for many jobs today are sold on a 'package' basis. You may well be prepared to forego hard cash, for instance, for something equally tangible, such as a company car. And if you are writing for a job which, at the time, does not exist, do provide some guide as to what salary you would expect. Prospective employers need to categorise you and can most easily do so via a salary band. Do not keep them guessing!

It is not a bad idea to keep a file of all jobs advertised in your area of search which, over a period, will provide the best guide of all to where you should be setting your sights. Surveys are published regularly, particularly in *The Financial Times*, of lower, median and upper salary levels paid across the entire field of career opportunities. As a guide to different management rewards, based upon the most senior manager below director level, the following lists these in order, with the highest paid function heading the list:

Legal advisors
General management
Advertising and public relations
Scientific departments
Finance and accounting
Marketing
Company secretaries
Computing
Personnel
Sales
Research and development
Administration
Distribution
Purchasing
Engineering
Quality assurance
Management services
Production
Architects and surveyors

This will, of course, change from time to time depending upon the laws of supply and demand and should be used as a guide only if you are contemplating a switch of function.

How Long Should You Set Yourself?

You will need patience, buckets of it, at least at first, for finding a *better* job is a far different task from finding a different job.

Back in 1973 the average length of unemployment was 11 weeks; by 1978 it had lengthened to 17 weeks and in 1983 was almost 26 weeks. Today it is beginning to reduce again, thanks to an improving economy, but the wait will still be there. Four deciding factors will determine just how long your wait is likely to be:

1. Whether or not you are currently employed;
2. Your age;
3. The salary level you are seeking; and
4. Possibly, the time of year.

As far as the first factor is concerned, we have already stated that it is a fact of life that someone already in a job is more easily placed in alternative employment than someone on the register of unemployed. If you are in this position, just face up to it.

Up to the age of 35, greater opportunities will present themselves, especially if you have made wise use of that period of your life. Thirty six may not sound old, but for each year over the 'magic' figure of 35 you should add a week or two to the time it will take you to get resettled.

Thus a man or woman between the ages of 40 and 50 might conceivably take three or four months longer to find acceptable alternative employment than someone 10 years their junior. Over the age of 50 it becomes progressively more difficult, for employers appear reluctant to add to their workforce people with, say, 10 to 15 years to retirement.

But if you are in this category, do not despair! As long as you have convinced *yourself* that you are not over the hill, you are in a strong position to convince others.

There will, of course, be the lucky few who will walk straight into something better. Qualifications, experience or simply a heightened demand for certain skills will assist easy mobility between careers. But do not bank on it.

The higher the salary bracket you are seeking, then the longer the wait is likely to be. Vacancies for chairmen of public companies or utilities do not crop up everyday and, even when they do, the jobs are usually filled through 'head hunters', agencies specialising in finding suitable candidates for prime positions.

The final factor, seasonality, will affect certain trades and professions in particular, although during the August holiday season and again near Christmas, employers are reluctant to find time for interviewing and may postpone filling vacancies until later.

As a general guide for the executive aged around 40, between 6 and 12 months should be allocated to the job hunt.

Consider splitting the waiting time into specified segments, as follows:

1. Taking stock of yourself — perhaps three or four weeks;
2. Planning your approach — a couple of weeks;
3. Considering any retraining needs, where the time will depend upon your requirements;
4. Researching the market place — another three or four weeks;
5. Writing your c.v. — a day or two;
6. Replying to advertisements — this will take until you are successful!

You will see that the total waiting period will vary according to individual situations, although an initial 'working phase' of around two months will help you prepare your challenge more thoroughly.

You may wish to set your own timing from the start, especially if other considerations come into the formula. Children's schooling, in particular, needs taking into account if your better job is likely to result in a house move. Finding a house you like and coupling this with 'suitable' schooling can be a protracted exercise, demanding both time and patience.

What is it Going to Cost?

Finding a better job is going to cost money. Some indication of the total can be gained by running through the following check-list and deciding for yourself how much you are prepared to spend in each category.

Further reading;
Purchasing newspapers and magazines advertising in the job sectors you are aiming at;
Writing paper, envelopes and postage;
Telephone calls;
Travelling to interviews where this is not refunded;
Counselling.

A budget is not a bad idea at this stage which can always be revised as you go along. We have ignored the fact that you might be out of work now and have to maintain yourself, and perhaps a family, for an indefinite period. These costs will, of course, be far greater, but even basic expenditure on the items listed above can quickly become substantial and it is better to be prepared for this before you start.

Keeping Records

Any task carried out methodically will result in a better end job and this golden rule applies just as much to your career search as to anything else.

At this stage you should already have several completed sheets of paper relating to your own personal analysis and these should be filed in a sensible order either in a plastic or manila folder under a suitable heading.

Your 'objectives' sheet should remain on top and be used as a constant reference source. These are the principles against which each and every avenue you consider taking should be carefully measured. If a course which initially appeals clashes with those basic requirements to which you have devoted careful thought, then think again. This is not to say that those objectives have to be set in cement, for they should indeed remain flexible, but before changing any of them consider the implications and ask yourself whether you might be losing sight of an important horizon for short-term gain.

Copies of your c.v., which we will look at in detail in Chapter 7, should form part of your pack.

If you can, set aside a desk top, or somewhere similarly suitable, where you can retain your papers and files in a neat and orderly fashion. Arm yourself with scissors, pens, plain paper, envelopes, stamps and your own research information. A nearby telephone point would be an asset, as would local business directories.

Every job advertisement to which you reply needs to be recorded and this can be done either on separate sheets of paper or by using white cards.

The original advertisement, its date and source, should be clipped to the sheet or card which should record:

Company name, address, telephone number, contact name;
Job description, location, salary, other benefits;
Any notes of your own;
Date responded and any follow-ups, i.e. telephone calls, interviews, etc.

A copy of your written reply should also be clipped to the record, as should any responses. If you attend an interview but are unsuccessful, try and add a few notes as to what went wrong, if anything, and any tips which you feel would be beneficial at subsequent interviews.

You should also have carried out some pre-interview research on the company you are to visit and this should be kept carefully with the other items. It may well be possible, at a later stage, to use this information in a 'cold call' approach by letter if you believe you have something special to offer that particular business.

With luck your records will not become too bulky but, being realistic, prepare yourself with a cabinet or suitable drawer to keep them in. Use them regularly, for a pattern should soon emerge which you can check against your basic requirements to ensure you stay on the right path. It is quite easy to stray, especially after a longish spell of disappointing applications and you may find yourself chasing jobs which do not really match up to your original expectations.

Make effective use of the time you have available and, preferably, set aside a period each day for your job hunt. Discipline is essential, especially into your second or third month if you remain unsuccessful in your search, for it is so much easier to switch on the television than to sit down and write yet another application. Determination will pay off!

Surveying the Market Place

You may well be fairly familiar with the job scene. Many perfectly contented employees still scan the advertisements on a regular basis, if only out of interest. It keeps them abreast of demand, pay levels and other benefits offered, as well as new areas of activity being pursued by major companies.

But if it has not been your habit to do this regularly, then you must allocate some early research time to catch up on new developments.

You will benefit from four areas of study:

1. Identifying which sectors of the market are most likely to expand and thus create greater job opportunities;
2. Using your local library, especially the reference section;
3. Regular studies of national and local newspapers, as well as pertinent trade magazines; and
4. Using your contacts.

Some crystal ball gazing may be necessary to seek out those sectors of industry and commerce likely to 'take off' over the next decade or so, although there are certain pointers and a recent survey highlighted, in particular, computers, accountancy, consumer services, leisure industries and high technology.

Another indicator is the demand by British applicants for undergraduate courses in UK universities; the latest statistics point to the following in order or popularity:

1. Law
2. Medicine
3. Management studies
4. English
5. History
6. Economics
7. Psychology (scientific and social)
8. Geography (scientific and social)
9. Computer studies
10. Mathematics
11. Biology
12. Chemistry
13. Pharmacy
14. Accountancy
15. Physics
16. Mechanical engineering

17. Electronic engineering
18. Sociology
19. General engineering
20. Civil engineering

You can see immediately that there are 'discrepancies' between this list and the earlier sectors referred to as likely leaders so do not believe everything you read! Such reports are no more than pointers, and your own feel of the market gained from topical study is the safest way forward.

Your library, especially if it is a large, modern one, should provide a wealth of reading, normally including a good selection of magazines. These are well worth studying, especially if they are new to you, for they may provide opportunities otherwise hidden.

To locate information on particular companies, any of the following will prove helpful:

Jordan Dataquest Ltd. (financial information on 40,000 companies in the fields of electronics, office equipment, data processing and chemicals);

Guide to Key British Enterprises (alphabetic listing of 20,000 prominent companies, along with their 'vital statistics');

Major Companies of Europe (Vol. 1: Continental EEC, Vol. 2: UK, Vol. 3 Non-EEC; 8,000 of the largest companies) 1988, Graham & Trotman, London;

Kelly's Directories UK (various classifications), Kelly's Directories, East Grinstead;

Stock Exchange Official Year Book (all quoted companies), Macmillan, London;

Who Owns Whom (UK edition) (a directory of parent, associate and subsidiary companies), 1987, Unwin Brothers Ltd., Woking;

Kompass UK (a registry of British industry and commerce), 1988, Kompass Publishers, East Grinstead.

Add to this general research any specific information you have gained on companies of your choice and make your own mind up about where the best job opportunities lie based upon what you have gleaned.

Newspapers must be read avidly — both the editorial content and the advertisements — for together they will provide both background and detailed information of the kind you are seeking. Some of the dailies, in particular the *Daily Telegraph*, *The Times* and *The Financial Times*, allocate certain days of the week to recruitment advertising and these you cannot afford to miss.

Study *Willings Press Guide*, published annually by British Media

Publications, for details of specialised magazines within those sectors you are looking to be placed. Many can then be scanned at larger newsagents before deciding upon which should be ordered on a regular basis.

Other sources of information might include:

Citizens' Advice Bureaux;
'Yellow Pages' or similar directories;
Employment agencies;
Job centres;
'The Hay Index', a quarterly report giving details of demand by function.

The final area to attack could prove to be the most beneficial, especially if you have access to a wide circle of colleagues and acquaintances connected with your area of search. This is the time to search your memory, track them down and seek their advice.

One thing you must not do, though, is to ask them for a job, for this could prove embarrassing to both of you. By all means ask if there is any way in which they can help, but only as a listening post, giving guidance or perhaps suggesting contacts of theirs to you who might be able to assist. Remember that many managerial posts are never advertised, as many as 50 per cent in some sectors and a very much greater proportion at the more senior levels. They are filled by word of mouth on the 'old boy' grapevine and there is no reason at all why you should not latch on to this method.

Fill a sheet of paper with names of:

Friends, neighbours, relatives and their positions in their companies;
Any professional friends, such as accountants, solicitors and the like, for these sort of people move in very wide circles and get to know a great number of acquaintances;
People connected with your present post, be they colleagues, customers or suppliers;
Former colleagues who have moved elsewhere or even those who have retired;
Any others with whom you are associated through membership of sporting or business clubs.

Once you have completed your list, place the names in order of priority, basing this upon how helpful you feel each might be in guiding you towards a better job. Clearly you must, at this stage at least, strike out anyone with whom you feel unable to share your news; this may include close colleagues at work if you are not yet ready to make your search public knowledge.

Each should then be approached, but in a 'formal', and certainly not a casual, manner. A casual enquiry is unlikely to produce the sort of positive stance that you are seeking. Instead, either arrange to meet for, say, half an hour at a place and time convenient to the other party or, if you feel it more appropriate, write a suitable letter.

. Whichever method is used, it should be tackled in the same manner. Prepare the ground thoroughly and know before you meet, or write, exactly how you intend to put your case. He is probably a busy person but likely to listen to you courteously and quietly. Do not waste his time, or yours, so outline in a structured manner:

Your reasons for seeking a better job;
What sort of career pattern you have in mind;
Your present experience and qualifications.

That is as far as you should go. As a round-up, simply say that you would welcome his guidance and if there is anyone he knows who could perhaps help further, you would very much appreciate the name or names.

Let him decide how long the 'interview' should take and make sure you detect any signs which he might make that it is at an end. Do not follow up these chats unless he has made it clear that you should do so.

Finally, all the time you are carrying out your researches, try and get other people to talk about *their* jobs because there is no better way to obtain a feel for other careers than in listening to those occupied in them. Most people enjoy talking about their jobs, even if they do not actually enjoy the job itself, and in encouraging them to provide you with details, you will gain knowledge at first hand which is not available in any text book.

Looking at Alternatives

Finding a better job might involve:

Actively seeking promotion with your present company;
Working part-time, or even flexi-hours;
Working for yourself; or
Working abroad.

The first of these clearly demands a different approach, although much of what you have learned so far will apply. Additionally, you will have to find out how you might qualify for a better post and it is normally wise to make your wishes known to your employer; he may be looking for someone just like you!

Working part-time, especially if the hourly rate is better than you now receive, has several advantages including:

Allowing you to continue to seek other employment;
Providing you with alternative experience;
Enabling you to meet a whole new set of people; and
Free time for other activities.

Many occupations cater for part-time work, including teachers and lecturers, librarians, social and health workers, lawyers, telephonists, and administrative staff. Employers find it more convenient and it can often help to fill those gaps in service industries where demand is at its peak.

More and more firms are moving to flexi-time where, as long as an employee works a set number of hours each week or month, he can come and go as he pleases. It is not, in fact, quite as flexible as this in practice, for there is always a 'core' period, say 10 a.m. to 4 p.m., when the employee has to be present. Nevertheless, it is a very popular system, especially in the insurance industry, and again allows you free time if you are casting your net around for something better.

Becoming self-employed may indeed prove to be that better job you have always sought, but this calls for an entirely different approach which will be looked at in Chapter 11.

Finding work overseas can be akin to starting life anew and this will stretch your researches even further, something that will be studied in Chapter 10.

But let us next try and review your qualifications and experience to see if a little retraining will enhance your chances of finding that better job.

CHAPTER 5

Retraining for a Fresh Start

The most positive way of effecting a successful career change is to take time out, sign yourself up for a whole new experience and start all over again.

This, of course, is fine if you are relatively young, have all the time in the world and a second income to enjoy. With family commitments and hungry mouths to feed it is a different story, but it can still be done.

Hardships there will be and you may have to carry your 'team' along with you, but perseverance can win you the day and, at the end of the tunnel, a better job and a better life. It is down to you.

The Government has recently announced a £15 million package to assist universities, polytechnics and colleges to invest in future training programmes aimed at encouraging people to update their skills throughout their working lives. Two million adults a year are expected to take part in what is known as the 'Pickup' Programme.

Whatever job you already hold, you can, of course, improve your status through self-training via a whole variety of methods, including:

- Residential establishments;
- Government or privately run colleges;
- Correspondence courses;
- Self-tuition;
- Specialised courses and institutions.

Few vocations are debarred from self-improvement and whilst your present employer may not encourage, or even allow, you to go along this path, the job market is becoming competitive enough for you to seek pastures new and a more enlightened boss.

Use this approach — your keenness to uplift your status through additional qualifications — when applying for that better job and this could put you ahead of the queue.

Hundreds of professional bodies exist with examination prospectuses geared to your requirements and, whilst studying will naturally take time, those magic letters to be gained and added after your name will be well worth the effort. They will stand out when prospective candidates are compared and give a personnel officer confidence in selecting you in preference to others less committed.

Whatever field you are operating in, it should be possible to take yourself that one important step ahead of your colleagues through an appropriate qualification.

Few are debarred. Secretaries planning to be high fliers, for example, can join the Institute of Qualified Private Secretaries, the letters IQPS adding value to their experience and any other qualifications. Moving from there into the world of lawyers, formal training leading to the Legal Secretaries' Certificate qualification means another step up the ladder to success — and possibly a better job.

Look around for the qualifications which really mean something in your present occupation, or the one you wish to enter. Get ahead in the race!

The Biggest Step

Whilst a great deal of retraining can be fitted in to an existing working life, the demands which it makes can be stressful in themselves and hamper the learning process. Thousands have achieved their ambition of adding to their knowledge and have successfully moved on to better things.

Relatives and friends have been sympathetic, allowing studying to progress alongside a background of family demands and life's natural hindrances. It is not easy, and no one would claim that it was so. But it is far easier, of course, to remove the working environment and allow the student to devote his whole time to the procurement of that additional knowledge that he desires. Our universities and polytechnics allow just that.

If, therefore, you believe you have the opportunity to go for a full-blooded training programme, then give very serious consideration to a degree course. There will naturally be entry qualifications and this hurdle will have to be taken first; these will normally consist of two or three 'A' level examinations which a few basic enquiries will clarify.

Your next step is to obtain the first class brochure published by the Universities Central Council on Admissions, commonly referred to as 'UCCA'.

UCCA was established in 1961 by the universities themselves to solve some of the problems arising from the increased pressure of applicants for admissions. It is managed by a Council of Management on which all the universities in the UK, except the Open University (dealt with separately later), the University of Buckingham and Cranfield Institute of Technology, are represented. It controls and centralises the admission to all universities represented, allowing candidates the freedom to make a responsible choice and at the same time allowing each university freedom to select its own students.

It does not provide academic advice such as which university to choose or entrance requirements but, once you have made up your mind on your favourites, it takes over. It can be found at PO Box 28, Cheltenham, Gloucestershire, GL50 1HY.

Its handbook provides basic details of all courses at the 44 or so universities in the UK leading to a first degree or a first diploma. A first degree is normally a bachelor's degree, such as BA, BSc, or LLB, although in Scotland the MA is a first degree. A few MEng courses are also covered.

Mature candidates are welcomed and should provide an account of their experience, employment history and any other relevant factors when applying including reasons why, if they prefer, they want to study at a university. A separate brochure entitled 'Mature Students and Universities' is available, free of charge, from UCCA.

You may be lucky enough to obtain a sponsor. Details of sponsorships available are published by the Employment Department Training Agency; whilst grant possibilities are covered by two booklets:

'Grants to Students', available from DES Publications Despatch Centre, Government Buildings, Honey Pot Lane, Stanmore, Middlesex, HA7 1AZ; and

'Guide to Students' Allowance', from Scottish Education Department, Awards Branch, Haymarket House, Clifton Terrace, Edinburgh, EH12 5DT.

Hobsons Publishing PLC, Bateman Street, Cambridge, CB2 1LZ publish a book on sandwich courses. If you are interested in combining or alternating university study with industrial or professional training, consult the university of your choice before writing to UCCA.

A fairly straightforward application form has to be sent to UCCA but generally up to 12 months before you wish to start your studies, so a degree of forward planning is essential!

The availability of courses at UK universities is extremely wide and runs from Sanskrit to Electronic Design and from Thai to Church History, with every variation between! The UCCA booklet provides details of all of these and is well worth studying before you commit yourself to any one course of study. In any event, consider taking a relatively wide-ranging rather than a highly specialised course unless you have set your sights on a particularly narrow avenue.

As well as the universities there are hundreds of polytechnics and colleges spread around the country offering an equally wide variety of new prospects. Here the central body is the Council for National Academic Awards (CNAA), the largest single degree-awarding body in the UK, and responsible for the courses designed, taught and examined in institutions of higher education such as polytechnics, institutes of higher education, colleges of art, colleges of technology and Scottish central institutions, which are not universities in their own rights. The degrees awarded by CNAA are recognised by employers, professional institutes and universities as equivalent in standard to university degrees and currently there are some 200,000 students in 130 institutions enrolled on over 2,000 CNAA approved courses.

As with universities, the content of these courses varies from college to college, but emphasis is placed upon providing student counselling, and practical ability is highly valued. Project work is encouraged and may take the form of practically-based projects or dissertations which contribute to the final award. Colleges are encouraged to angle their courses towards the needs of industry, commerce and the professions.

Most CNAA courses follow the standard pattern of three years' full-time study, but many are sandwich courses combining academic study with supervised work experience. There are also part-time courses.

Whilst fairly stringent academic qualifications are sought for admission in the case of school-leavers, there is far greater flexibility for mature students, i.e. those aged over 21. You should obtain from CNAA's Publications Unit, 344–354 Gray's Inn Rd., London, WC1X 8BP a copy of 'Opportunities in Higher Education for Mature Students'.

If you can convince a college that you are interested in and capable of sustained study, then you are eligible for special consideration for entry to a full-time, sandwich or part-time undergraduate course leading to one of the following CNAA awards:

- Bachelor of Arts (BA);
- Bachelor of Science (BSc);
- Bachelor of Education (BEd);
- Diploma of Higher Education (Dip HE).

Choosing the most appropriate course is, naturally, essential and you are well advised to make contact with your local polytechnic or college to discuss this before you get too far down the road to making a decision. Study, remember, will still be demanding and you need to be sure that you have the time, money and motivation to undertake a course which is bound to have moments of pressure, such as when essay deadlines have to be met or examinations taken, which may impinge upon family demands.

Subjects run into hundreds and a directory of these is available from CNAA as above which also lists the dozens of teaching institutions which are affiliated.

You will normally qualify for a mandatory grant for a full-time course unless you have previously pursued a course of higher education, or if you cannot fulfil certain residential requirements, or you are attending certain privately funded colleges. Make enquiries at an early stage of your local education authority.

Before leaving the field of full-time study, take a close look at the possibility of gaining a Master's Degree in Business Administration, or MBA. This is normally a one year course of study run by the country's top management colleges such as Ashridge and the City University Business School in London. It is particularly appropriate for people who have gained both general and specific experience in a working environment and who are then keen to progress into the higher echelons of management. A firm grounding in analytical technique and strategic thinking is provided, and, in addition to the core of central studies which accounts for about half of the course, each student selects a particular area of expertise such as export management, international business, marketing, industrial relations or finance. Tuition is intense (forget a nine to five day!) and the volume of required reading, research and course work especially testing. Leadership skills head up a whole host of managerial techniques taught and there is little doubt that a potential employee boasting an MBA qualification is taken very seriously.

Part-time Study

Opportunities remain unlimited in this country for anyone wishing to expand their knowledge. Only a few hours a week dedicated to the specialist subject of your choice allows you the freedom to participate in new areas, opening up fresh horizons and widening for you the sphere of job possibilities.

Hundreds of colleges in almost every major conurbation lay there waiting for you to sign on, eager to communicate new skills. The sheer number of possible courses becomes a daunting prospect in itself, however, and another military style operation is called for to prevent you chasing down inopportune avenues.

Begin, not with the prospectus, but with your defined list of objectives. Browsing through a myriad of topics will deflect your positive thinking and put you in danger of electing for an attractive course in landscape painting instead of one to further your career!

Scour the area to find out what different colleges have to offer and look not just at traditional teaching methods but at some of the new ones which make full use of modern technology, including home videos and personalised tutorial packs.

Get hold of 'The Open Book', a guide to Open College courses published by The Open College, Suite 470, St. James's Buildings, Oxford Street, Manchester, M1 6FQ. Claiming to be the fastest growing training establishment in Europe, the Open College makes use of existing educational establishments to provide people with new skills and abilities, and is encouraged by the Government. Open Learning methods are used, giving you the opportunity to choose when, where, and how to study. You proceed at your own pace and at a time and place that suits you best. Appropriate materials are provided and it is then up to you to decide how you want to do the work; ideal for someone already in full-time employment. A national network of Open Access Centres exist where you can obtain help and advice, and join the College; a 'hotline' on 0235-555444 (in Scotland 041-334-3141) is available to tell you your nearest Access Centre.

There are over 50 courses under the headings of Getting Started,

Business and Management, Industry and Technology, Service Skills, Practical Skills and In and Out of Work. Course material is interesting, practical and yours to keep for ever; it includes:

- Workbooks
- Resource books
- Practical kits
- Audio tapes
- Video tapes
- Computer software
- Assignment books

Alongside the practical work are Channel 4 programmes, generally transmitted at lunch times.

Some of the courses currently available are:

- The Woman Manager (for women wanting to take up managerial posts);
- Understanding Information Technology;
- How to Make Money Out of Your Pub (in conjunction with the British Institute of Innkeeping);
- An Introduction to Effective Selling (in conjunction with the Institute of Sales and Marketing Management);
- Practical Child Care;

and many, many others. Some colleges are advertising this method of teaching under 'Flexistudy'. Make enquiries locally.

Several universities are offering Open Studies programmes and although many of the courses are leisure related, keep your eye open for specialist subjects especially aimed at those wishing to further their careers. Lessons are held at centres of education and elsewhere (some in castles!) within the vicinity of the organising university.

Several management colleges specialise in career development, amongst them Cranfield School of Management, Cranfield, Bedford, MK43 OAL, which has a depth of experience in the subject and caters for managers' needs at various stages of development. Its specialised courses include the Young Manager's Programme, Management Development Programme, General Management for Specialists and a Programme for Senior Managers.

Henley is another management college offering sound, practical experience of business environment both on a residential basis and through the Distance Learning concept; speak to them at Greenlands, Henley on Thames, Oxon, RG9 3AU. The Manchester Business School, Booth Street West, Manchester, M15 6PB, Ashridge Management College, Berkhamsted, Hertfordshire, HP4 1NS, and Insead, 77305 Fontainbleau Cedex, France are other similar institutions with a long history of teaching management techniques.

Other colleges offer specialist tuition in subjects as diverse as engineering, computer studies, secretarial skills and accountancy. You will find in any good reference library directories of these, most of which are run on a commercial basis and therefore charge fees appropriately. Before enrolling with a college not known to you, make suitable enquiries within their field of knowledge to ensure they are legitimate; regrettably there do exist a few 'institutions' which are not all that they claim to be. It is important that the piece of paper with which you finish up is universally recognised.

Correspondence Courses

Before embarking on one of these, think carefully through the implications of not being able to put questions directly to a tutor, although some colleges do include an annual seminar for face-to-face sessions. Questions can, of course, be returned by post, but by the time you receive the answer, others will have no doubt sprung to mind!

Some students find they cannot cope with this type of faceless tuition; others have found it very effective, enabling them to fit in their studies precisely when they wish. Try to define your own category before signing on!

In any event, obtain a list of those colleges accredited for correspondence by the Council for the Accreditation of Correspondence Colleges, 27 Marylebone Road, London, NW1 5JS, which was formed in 1969 as an independent body with the co-operation of the Secretary of State for Education and Science who nominates experienced educationalists for the Council. Standards are set for all aspects of postal tuition and a college is not given accredited status unless it conforms with these standards.

Only about 40 colleges in the UK are entitled to CACC status, but these offer a wide variety of topics covering both general and specific subjects. Three examples are:

The Rapid Results College, Tuition House, 27/37 St. George's Road, London, SW19 4Ds, which offers professional examinations in accountancy, banking, computing, finance, management, marketing, transport, etc., as well as basic educational courses, a law degree and police promotion examinations.

Transworld Education College, 8 Elliot Place, Clydeway Centre, Glasgow, G3 8EF, which specialises in providing courses to enable you to obtain a better job. Building, electronics, personnel management, agriculture, engineering and business management are just a few examples.

National Extension College, 18 Brooklands Avenue, Cambridge, CB2 2HN, is an educational charity with 25 years of experience of providing a high quality comprehensive service to correspondence students and was established to provide second chance education for adults. Its 300 or so tutors are active in universities, colleges and schools and there are flexistudy links with local colleges.

The Open University

Tens of thousands of people can testify to the fact that their lives have been changed, often dramatically, by the use of this particular teaching medium.

The Open University was founded by Royal Charter in 1969 with the aim of providing educational opportunities for adults preferring, or only able, to study in their own homes and in their own time. It adopts a multi-media approach to teaching, including the use of television, video, audio cassettes, correspondence and face-to-face tuition, and has been judged one of the most important innovations ever in the British educational system.

It uses 13 regional centres to provide nationwide coverage and over 250 study centres exist for the use of students. Over 70,000 adults have already gained full degrees by this method.

The Open University offers a superb opportunity to further your chances of securing that better job with a whole range of courses with this objective specifically in mind. These are of varying lengths and types and include areas such as computing, engineering, management, health and the social services. Some lead to an academic qualification while others provide updating, but all are specialised and relevant to professionals and have been designed primarily for those who have had practical experience in a given field and who wish to develop or broaden their skills or understanding to a higher level.

The amount of previous experience or knowledge required will vary from course to course, although many assume no previous experience at all. Be careful, though, to ensure that you can cope with a particular course before enrolling.

You can choose from a range of about 130 courses, with the intention of gaining 'half credits' or 'full credits' until you have enough to qualify for the Bachelor of Arts degree. This is likely to take you between three and six years to complete, and perhaps a little longer for a BA (Honours) degree where eight full credits are needed as opposed to six. The degree can be either arts or science based and is recognised as being equivalent in every way to a full degree from any other British university.

The time necessary can be reduced if you are granted 'advanced standing' in recognition of successful previous study at higher educational level. And if you already hold a degree, the Open University offers the opportunity to take a taught or research based higher degree.

Studying at home, of course, requires a great deal of willpower — and the support of family and friends. Planning your studies around other activities will not be easy, but the outcome can be very rewarding, as thousands have already found.

Each course lasts, normally, from February until October and, for a full credit course, you may be spending up to 14 hours each week studying.

It is a big step, and will cost you money. Fees can, however, be paid in instalments and your local education authority may help. Employers, also, are sometimes keen to assist with finance, especially if they see you moving up in their operation.

The regional centres are eager to talk things over with you prior to commitment and your nearest can be found by contacting the Open University at PO Box 71, Milton Keynes, MK7 6AG.

The Open Business School

This is part of the Open University and one of the largest providers of management education in the country, offering a wide range of distance taught short courses covering every aspect of management. It was set up in 1983 since when over 18,000 registrations have been received from managers in all sectors of industry and commerce. In addition, some 2,500 companies and organisations have shown their confidence in the School by sponsoring participants. One of these is the British Institute of Management which makes a number of bursaries available each year on The Effective Manager course. Details are obtainable from the BIM, Management House, Cottingham Road, Corby, Northants, NN17 1TT.

Because of its popularity, the School has since established its own School of Management as a full faculty of the University able to offer students increased opportunities in management education and research, including an MBA degree. Fees are modest, and the courses are flexible enough to form part of company training programmes or be enhanced by in-house sessions.

No formal entrance qualifications are called for and anyone living in the UK (or, indeed, in Belgium, Luxembourg, the Republic of Ireland or at a BFPO address in Europe) aged over 18 can apply to the Open University address above.

The length of courses varies between about 8 weeks and 30 weeks, with some three to five hours of weekly study necessary; The Effective Manager course takes a little longer. The study time can include attending tutorials and completing written assignments. Multi-media tuition is provided in a similar way to that used by the Open University.

Several professional bodies have recognised certain of the courses provided as being eligible for part exemptions from their examinations, including the Institute of Personnel Management and the Institute of Marketing. Make certain, first, that you understand eligibility before committing yourself to a particular course if your aim is to gain a professional qualification.

Women into Management is precisely what it says and is an eight week course especially for women who want to enter, or return to, a management career.

The Open Business School is fully recognised by industry and commerce and boasts an impressive 'client' list which includes the BBC, British Airways, Courtaulds, Ferranti, GEC, ICI, Royal Insurance, Texaco, United Kingdom Atomic Energy Authority and many others.

Still at Home

We have taken a look at a variety of home-based tuition courses organised by professional institutes, but it is still possible to 'teach yourself' without leaving the comfort of your armchair and, more importantly, without undue cost. What is essential, though, is a great deal of willpower.

Books on every subject under the sun are readily available from your local library and, with a carefully planned programme over a set period, you should be able to raise your qualification level to a desired standard.

Certainly, professional qualifications can be gained via this method although it may take a little longer than using a traditional correspondence course. If you have the time — and the incentive — it could be worth the investment. Seek out the recommended reading books and, alongside these, study past examination papers normally obtainable from the relevant professional body. Check out employment requirements at the start to make quite certain you are eligible.

Television and radio programmes, such as those aimed at Open University students, can help, although almost certainly they will have to be backed up by written material.

These methods are suitable only for those with the determination to succeed, following a period of cautious research, and are unlikely to prove the right method for someone requiring regular prompting and encouragement.

Across the Language Barrier

In a recent survey a British company was asked how it overcame the language barrier when negotiating with foreign customers. 'We shout loudly in English' was the reply!

One of the most marketable commodities in employment is the fluent usage of a foreign language, and it is not as difficult as you might think to gain this expertise. Admittedly, it will take a lot of midnight hours — some 300 to 400 may be needed to get you to intermediate level — but the satisfaction in being able to converse in a tongue other than your own natural one will make it all worthwhile. And, as far as job searching goes, it will without doubt ease the path.

The Europeans and the Japanese, in particular, have led the way in providing their export ambassadors with the ability to speak in English and, if we are to compete successfully, we must follow that lead.

If you have a basic, even schoolday, knowledge of French or German, then start with that. You may be able to cut out a lot of the initial tutorials and even surprise yourself at how quickly you can progress. Some people, of course, are more adept at learning a new language than others, but until you try you will not really know. Do not be put off by early difficulties; set yourself a realistic time target by which you are able to read and speak basic sentences and then take further progress a step at a time.

Visiting the country of your choice and listening to, as well as speaking that language will move your learning on by leaps and bounds. The accents and intonations of the French language, for example, can only be heard authentically in France.

For the basics, though, choose your method of study very carefully. Many early attendees of local college night classes find themselves frustrated after two or three sessions simply because the teaching level is either too basic or too advanced for them. If you intend to adopt this method, seek out the tutor before you book yourself in to find out precisely whether he is dealing with absolute beginners, those with a little knowledge or those already near-fluent and wishing to improve themselves further.

Language schools, either residential or on a distance learning basis, shout their claims from every newspaper, but take some of these with a large pinch of salt. To speak Spanish, say, from a standing start in just three and a half weeks is going to take an awful lot of willpower!

Nevertheless, to give the better language schools credit, many of them allow you to test their wares for a week or two, guaranteeing your money back if you are not fully satisfied. Using the 'correspondence' method of learning, as we have suggested before, may not be for you and, in the case of acquiring new language skills, the absence of a tutor to answer queries can present difficulties.

You have nothing to lose, however, with a reputable company which offers you its 'money back' guarantee, and a week or two of disciplined dedication could pay handsome dividends.

Forget, incidentally, the boring methods by which you might have learned basic French or German at school; today's language schools are very switched on to the latest psychological means of feeding input into your brain! They make it far more palatable, often using the subconscious coupled with background music to speed along your learning process!

The BBC, through both radio and television media, offer useful language courses alongside specialist books and cassettes which can be purchased beforehand. A selection of what is available at any one time might include:

Chinese
Turkish
Spanish
Italian
German
Russian
French

'Teaching as a New Career'

This is the title of a booklet issued by TASC, Room 4/17 Elizabeth House, York Road, London, SE1 7PH aimed at attracting men and women with practical industrial or commercial experience back into the classrooms.

There exists a continuing demand for good teachers in all subjects, but particularly in mathematics, physics, craft, design and technology, and business studies. Language teachers will also be required following the adoption of a national curriculum in the early 1990s.

In order to teach in a state-maintained school you must be a qualified teacher. The most common route to this status is through successful completion of an approved course of initial teacher training (ITT) in an English or Welsh institution. The main types of ITT course are the Post Graduate Certificate in Education or the Bachelor of Education.

Graduates can thus pursue the former via a one year Certificate in Education course which will include supervised teaching practice and professional studies in teaching, but a relevant degree is normally necessary to qualify. Engineers, for instance, should be looking at a PGCE course in craft, design and technology, or physics. Some part-time courses are available.

For the Bachelor of Education you will have to set aside four years, although in some disciplines the time-scale is a little shorter, such as mathematics, physics, craft, design and technology and business studies. There are specially designed courses for mature, non-graduate entrants with the necessary professional qualifications and experience.

The Government is funding a bursary scheme to increase the supply of qualified teachers in certain defined subjects and students on PGCE courses are eligible for a flat rate tax free bursary in addition to the normal student grants.

If any of this sounds to you like your best route to a better job, there has never been a more opportune time to take advantage of what is on offer. Send for the booklet now.

Some Other Avenues

Consider joining the British Institute of Management (Management House, Parker Street, London, WC2B 5PT), which acts as a central body for the country's managers following its foundation in 1947 since when it has devoted itself exclusively to the development of the art and science of management.

Apart from being a powerhouse of information, the BIM also runs conferences, courses and seminars throughout the year at regular intervals in London and many other centres. A Careers Advisory Service is available to members, manned by experienced counsellors and with access to information on courses, placement agencies, vocational guidance centres and other sources of advice on career changes and development. The advice service is free to members although a charge is made for each counselling interview. Management House also contains one of the largest management libraries in the world with some 70,000 books, journals, pamphlets and company documents available for reference and borrowing.

Another body of interest to you at this important stage of your development might be the British Association for Commercial and Industrial Education, a voluntary non-political charity founded in 1919 and operating in the fields of vocational education and training. It can be found at 16 Park Crescent, London, W1N 4AP. BACIE is a member of the Employment Department Training Agency's voluntary registration scheme for the training of trainers and consequently maintains a Review Group which keeps an eye on this important aspect of education. Courses and workshops are designed on a modular basis to ensure maximum flexibility for those taking part, and courses may be taken at almost any time of the year.

Although mainly a corporate membership organisation, individuals are welcome to join and make use of the full membership services, including discounts on courses and free use of BACIE's comprehensive information service and library.

All courses and workshops are designed to ensure:

- The relevance of course focus by the use of pre-course questionnaires to establish the needs of each individual;

- Flexibility in continuing to meet the needs of people by the use of participative techniques and informal feedback during the training period;

- That learning is consolidated through a range of practical exercises and skill practice sessions;

- That learning is relevant and transfer is encouraged by use of individual projects, where appropriate, at the end of the event, and by the preparation of action plans;

- That feedback is provided to the tutor to help him assess progress on a continuing basis;

- Learning is transferred to the workplace by encouraging the student's manager to carry out pre- and post-course briefing sessions;

- That up-to-date thinking, techniques and developments in the training field are incorporated in all of the courses and workshops.

Tutors are selected for their depth of experience of the training subject and their skills as learning facilitators.

Courses are both residential and non-residential and are being constantly updated to meet the needs of industry and commerce. Aims for each are clearly set out as guidelines and an indication is provided as to the sort of people who would best gain from the sessions.

Finally, arm yourself with a copy of 'Your Guide to Our Employment, Training and Enterprise Programmes', published by the Department of Employment and obtainable from any job centre. This will guide you through the morass of assistance available through governmental sources and is sectionalised into:

Employment
Training
Enterprise
Special needs.

The first of these sections, for example, tells you how to apply for financial assistance towards attending job interviews, and also provides details of the Jobclub Scheme for those out of work for some time.

The section on training guides you along the paths of career development, obtaining grants, and where to start your search if you are contemplating running your own business or have already started one but with little success.

The Enterprise Allowance Scheme, Loan Guarantee Scheme, Business Expansion Scheme and similar possibilities are covered under Enterprise, whilst those with disabilities or within an ethnic minority are catered for under Special Needs.

Counselling and advice centres are listed and, all in all, it is one of the better brochures to have come out of the relevant government department for some time. Do not miss out on it!

These, then, are just a selection of the methods by which you are able to better your own chances of success before beginning the big search . . .

CHAPTER 6

Where to Start Looking

Although job advertisements come quickly to mind, they are in fact only one source of several in your search for that better job. But let us start with them . . .

Advertisements

Newspapers are the obvious first choice, but learn to be selective or your research funds will quickly dwindle! A library based study of all the major dailies over a period of a week will provide you with a clear indication of where you should be spending your money — or more time in the library!

All the quality nationals incorporate career advertisements but *The Times*, the *Guardian*, *Daily Telegraph* and the *Observer* shine above the rest, coupled with the thicker Sunday papers. Do not miss out, also, on evening editions of localised newspapers, whilst some of the weeklies carry good job features. At first it might seem a mammoth task but it should not take you too long to turn it into a science.

You do not have to read every advertisement. Learn to train your eye into discarding what will obviously be the majority, those, for instance, with a salary indicator tag reading 'Package £20,000 to £22,000' if your sights are set much higher, or vice versa as the case may be.

Many managerial vacancies are grouped together under a heading such as 'Accountancy Appointments' or 'Legal Positions Available' so that these, also, may be discarded unless that is what you are looking for.

Most, however, fall randomly across the pages and 'Senior Petroleum Products Trader' is just as likely to be next to 'Managing Director' or 'Business Analyst'. Flick across each page, from top to bottom, to seek out job titles which might attract you and which, of course, fall within the boundaries you have already set yourself. Resist the temptation to look deeper into advertisements which you know are not really for you but which nevertheless look interesting. Fascinating as 'Global Bank Director £100,000 p.a. plus many benefits' might be, your time is better occupied with selecting those advertisements more likely to provide you with the opportunity of meeting the objective of this book!

Look first at the job title. If this fits, look next for the sector such as 'Micro-electronics', 'High technology industrial sector' or 'British Flat Roofing Council'. Again, if this is outside your actual or intended field of experience, move on. If it appeals, seek out the geographical location which might be as specific as 'Canterbury' or 'Scotland', as vague as 'Southern England' or, in many cases, be completely absent.

If job title, salary, sector and area all appear to fit your plan, scan the remainder of the wording, although the next few words may well mean discarding it. Instances might be:

'Essential graduate background': do not bother applying unless you have this qualification;

'An experienced Sales Manager is required': you will be wasting everyone's time if you have no experience in this discipline at all;

'A sound knowledge of the building industry is required': this means precisely what it says;

'You should be under 40': an exceptional 41 year old might apply, but not someone nearer 45;

'At least five years experience in a manufacturing environment': four might just do, coupled with exceptional qualifications, but two will not.

Certainly there is no need to meet every requirement slavishly, but do explain yourself if you are seeking to obtain an interview in the absence of matching up precisely to the advertisement. Do not ignore the fact, face up to it and spell out your reasons.

In addition to the newspapers, study any relevant magazines and professional journals; the latter are especially suitable for many of the professions, including accountancy, law, banking and so on.

Four specialist newspapers to look out for are:

Executive Post: A weekly published by Professional and Executive Recruitment, 2 Fitzwilliam Gate, Sheffield, S1 4JH. Full of helpful advice, training course details, book reviews, etc., as well as containing details of dozens of vacancies. Budding entrepreneurs are also catered for, and the paper adds tips on forwarding job applications.

Recruitment Now (incorporating 'Candidate Focus'): Also published by PER and incorporating a guide to some 250 managerial, scientific and technically qualified job seekers. The editorial section provides a platform for the exchange of information and views on recruitment and matters directly concerning recruiters of executives, managers and other professional staff. Topics include salary movement indicators, developments in recruitment and selection, personality profiles of personnel heads and training matters.

Graduate Focus: Another PER publication in which graduates can advertise their availability, qualifications and salary levels sought.

Graduate Post: Published by The Newpoint Publishing Company Ltd., Newpoint House, St. James' Lane, London, N10 3DF, in association with PER. As well as a great deal of informative editorial, this newspaper contains hundreds of vacancies for graduates.

Where Else?

Providing you have 'gone public' on your desire to seek a better job, then make use of every available source, for lurking there somewhere could be just the vacancy you are after and, quite possibly, you may hear of it before it hits the papers.

Friends, relations, business colleagues and anyone else you can lay your hands on should be contacted and those most likely to be fruitful seen on a regular basis, as long as you do not outstay your welcome. Advice on the best approach was provided in Chapter 4 and you are now recommended to read that section again.

Register with both local and appropriate national employment agencies, after checking who specialises in what in the members list of the Federation of Recruitment and Employment Services, a copy of which is kept in larger libraries. Junior management posts, especially, are catered for by these agencies, although more senior positions are generally left to national advertising.

Keep your eye on the displays in your local job centre, where you can also obtain useful free advice and an indication of the job scene in the sector and location of your choice. Staff are generally very friendly and will give willingly of their time if a particular point is troubling you.

Professional associations may be able to help if you are already a member of one of these, the better ones offering counselling advice.

Another series of organisations to consider are what used to be known as 'head hunters', but today, more politely, 'Search and Selection Consultancies.' At any one time these will have a number of vacancies to fill on behalf of their employer clients, along with another list of people such as yourself looking for vacancies to fill. It is the consultants' job to match the two with maximum benefit to all three parties — and that will include a fairly large fee for themselves.

This fee, however, is generally payable by the lucky employer who sees his job space suitably filled. If you do have an impressive c.v., though, you will be welcomed by these agencies whose job you will be making a little easier. Personal counselling, of course, will cost you money and this is discussed later on.

Professional and Executive Recruitment (PER)

By now you will probably know about this body, originally government sponsored, and describing itself as Britain's largest executive recruitment consultancy. Through its very wide network it is able to put high-quality executives actively seeking a change of job in touch with employer clients seeking to fill posts. Its statistics are impressive, from turning over around 3,000 candidates each week from the largest bank of executive job seekers in the country, to dealing with over 250,000 executives each year.

PER runs job hunting seminars, normally half-day informal sessions designed to help executives needing to sharpen their job hunting and interview skills. Practical help is given in self- assessment and projection along with guidance on career direction and development.

Self-help groups, where known, are contained in a central register and The British Unemployment Resource Network, 318 Summer Lane, Birmingham, B19 6RL, keeps up-to-date lists of local groups.

PER has offices in some 35 locations throughout England, Wales and Scotland, and over 300 consultancy staff and most of the major national and multi-national corporations use its services.

A first-class publication entitled 'The Job Hunting Handbook' is available, without charge, from their Sheffield headquarters.

Counselling

Unlike 'head hunters' and selection consultants, executive counsellors work entirely in the individual's interest, helping him towards self-assessment and ultimately guiding him towards that job that is going to be both better and appropriate to his own development. Career counsellors are generally experienced former executives in their own right and their work is often backed up by occupational psychologists. Their specialist skills are particularly valuable in systematically developing all of the techniques of marketing you, the individual, and also taking into account the total situation and career of their clients, and their families.

Counselling firms tend to specialise in certain sectors of the market and some initial homework is necessary on your part before you sign up. Services can include preparation of your c.v. and assistance with self-advertising, if this is recommended.

You may opt for a self-assessment analysis on its own and this can be provided by The Independent Assessment and Research Centre, 57 Marylebone High St., London, W1 for a reasonable fee. Tests are usually taken during group sessions lasting up to a day, followed by an individual interview to hear and discuss the outcome. Help is provided, where appropriate, for clients to follow up on their own account any new lines of investigation which the exercise has highlighted.

The Vocational Guidance Association of 7 Harley House, Upper Harley Street, London, NW1 4RP, is the oldest established body devoted to vocational guidance in the world and was founded in 1954, originally to provide help for young people in schools and universities.

Over the years the Association's activities have extended to cover the full range of career counselling functions and people seeking a mid-career change are especially catered for. Branches also exist in Northampton, Liverpool, Cheltenham and Glasgow.

Consultations consist of firstly filling in a form providing your counsellor with educational and career details, followed by a visit to a VGA centre to take a series of written and visual tests lasting a couple of hours. You are asked several hundred questions, often presenting the same point in a different manner, in an effort to reveal your personal qualities of leadership, independence, attitudes to others and so on.

Many of the counsellors are occupational psychologists and, after a lapse of several weeks for papers to be analysed, you return to have a session with one of these. Results are presented in the form of graphs which are readily explained to you. Follow-up advice is available for the next two years without extra charge.

A specialist function of the VGA is 'Crisis Counselling', where you have undergone some trauma, such as:

Serious illness, of yourself or a close relative;
Emotional problems at home;
Drink problems, suspected or actual;
Emotional conflict within the work environment;
Team crises which have developed.

Equal Opportunities for All

If you feel you have been unfairly treated because of your sex in your job, your pay, or chances of promotion, you can look to help from the Equal Opportunities Commission who can be contacted at Overseas House, Quay Street, Manchester, M3 3HN.

The EOC is a public body set up by Parliament in 1975 to prevent people being treated unfairly simply because of their sex and, in the area of employment, to prevent discrimination against married people. You have three powerful Acts of Parliament on your side:

The Sex Discrimination Act, 1975;
A further version of this Act, passed in 1986; and
The Equal Pay Act, 1970.

Every case is considered individually and advice provided; in extreme cases the EOC will fight your case for you. The main drive, however, is to persuade the other party of his infringement of your rights, since using the powers of the law is not always the best way to achieve wholehearted co-operation.

Racial discrimination is, of course, equally covered by statute and, in either case if you feel aggrieved, see a good solicitor.

Just for Women

Although many jobs still pay less for women than for men, despite union and legal pressures, women are undoubtedly starting to break into top jobs.

A recent British Institute of Management research survey discovered that the number of women holding down management posts had doubled between 1986 and 1988. Even the number of female chief executives had also doubled during the same period.

They also enjoyed faster-rising salaries than their male counterparts, and it was found that, on average, women were up to six to eight years younger than men when they first moved into an executive post.

Overseas, it has been proved that British trained women do particularly well and in Japan, for instance, they are so rare that they have an automatic advantage, even if it is initially based on curiosity only! Feminine attributes of patience, tolerance and politeness go down exceptionally well abroad, especially in the Far East where these virtues form part of their inheritance.

Looking exclusively after women is the National Advisory Centre on Careers for Women, 8th Floor, Artillery House, Artillery Row, London, SW1P 1RT. This body is a registered charity formed in 1933 and has HM Queen Elizabeth the Queen Mother as its patron. Its objective is to provide vocational guidance for girls and women and it caters especially for the woman returning to work after a spell bringing up a family. Workshops are held to help develop your potential through study or a new interest, and the opportunity is provided to share ideas with others in a similar position.

Whilst it does not deal exclusively with women, Atlas Employment Ltd, Greater London's leading and fastest growing recruitment agency with 58 branches, does specialise in vacancies for women and has an all female board led by Managing Director, Anona O'Sullivan. Mrs. O'Sullivan takes a positive stance in meeting the needs of women returning to work in later life.

Specialist divisions of particular interest to women have been established in the fields of fashion, catering, accountancy and languages, the latter aiming directly at the implications of a closer Europe.

If you are in the London area, look in your telephone directory to find your nearest branch.

CHAPTER 7

Writing an Effective C.V.

Here is where you have to sell yourself completely 'blind'. Just as an advertisement needs to be attractive enough to induce you to go out and buy, so must your 'life story' make sufficient impact upon a prospective employer that, instead of discarding it along with dozens of others, he will sit up and take sufficient notice of it to give you a second thought. That is all, at this stage, that you are seeking. A second thought.

As many as 2,000 replies can be received for a cleverly worded job advertisement in one of the quality Sunday newspapers. Just imagine the task of sorting through those, knowing that, at the end of the day, only one will normally be chosen. Your c.v. will determine whether or not you are in the initial discard pile, or in the stalls along with several others with a chance of winning the Grand National. Those are the sort of odds against you — so make your c.v. work!

A 'curriculum vitae' means, literally, a 'schedule of your life', thus providing the reader with an instant picture of your past. Upon it he will make an instant decision.

If a recruitment agency is the recipient, they will usually spot the 'mass produced' c.v., the sort which indicates the more casual enquirer as opposed to the serious career changer. What you have to avoid, therefore, is falling into the first category by honing your own version to perfection. So let us see how to tackle this vital tool.

Producing the Perfect C.V.

What to call it is the first decision. There are schools of thought that suggest that, instead of simply c.v., such an important document deserves a longer title.

Some applicants like the full 'curriculum vitae', probably set in capitals and duly underlined. Others prefer words such as 'Resumé', 'Career History' or 'Details of . . .'. Yet another school of thought will tell you to call it nothing, to leave the front page blank, for the interior will tell it all without further clarification. It really does not matter. The busy employer, or job agency, is not going to read the title; he will be so used to such documents, that that part of it will make no impression upon him at all. He is after the meat!

Photographs are not really necessary, unless specifically requested. They add nothing materially to the story you have to tell although there will be the odd exception where you feel especially strongly that your visage smiling out of your document will swing a decision in your favour. Air hostesses and models apart, photographs are generally redundant.

Your c.v. should not be a tablet set in stone and it may well be appropriate to produce two or three variations. Much may depend upon the horizons you have set yourself and, if these are appropriately wide apart, then it may well be wise to have a version to fit each occasion.

Ideally, of course, you would write a c.v. for each job for which you applied but, in practice, no employer expects this ideal. Nevertheless, you should make yours sound as if it were custom built, for it will then have greater impact. Certainly the general tone of your c.v. must match the job description for it to stand any chance at all. One giving the impression, for instance, of a heavy engineering background, supported by matching qualifications and experience, is hardly likely to appeal to an employer seeking a body to fill his software department.

Similarly, over emphasis in certain areas will provide a reader with first impressions of the wrong variety if you are looking to a major shift to another field. Balance is thus a critical component of any effective c.v.

It is likely to be 'skip-read' in the first instance, just as you might have skip-read the chapter headings in this book before deciding to buy it. That first glance will have provided you with an impression, either favourable or otherwise, and it only takes a few seconds. It is very much like meeting a stranger; most of us come to instant conclusions before a dozen words are spoken yet, given time, those 'conclusions' invariably prove to be misfounded.

With a c.v., time is not on the reader's side. He has a busy schedule ahead of him and only first impressions are allowed an opportunity. For this reason, if no other, your c.v. should be kept short, ideally to no more than two sheets of A4 size paper. This is not an easy discipline. Most of us want to fill three or four sheets, sometimes more, but this must be avoided at all costs. Two sheets it must be, unless the circumstances are exceptional. It may start off longer than this. Then comes the cutting process, because remember that it must finish life as a readable document. One that will, for a fleeting moment or two, sit atop a pile of similar documents but one which, at that vital stage, you want to ensure is placed in the 'second chance' pile and not in the discard pack.

It must, therefore, be presentable as well as having the 'right' ingredients. Good quality, A4 paper is essential and, preferably, it should not be bent although, if envelope cost is going to be significant, two neat folds are allowed.

Should it be typed, computer-processed or printed? Any one of these is acceptable, although printed versions do tend to smack of permanency, as if you are expecting a long haul before landing the right job. Certainly it should not be handwritten.

If you can produce it neatly on a computer spread-sheet, and particularly if it is a computer related position you are after, then this may well be the most appropriate presentation.

A neatly typed c.v., however, takes some beating and, well-spaced and carefully planned, should not fail to catch the reader's eye if it also contains just what he is looking for.

What Should Be Included

There are no standard guidelines as to what should or should not be put into a c.v. It is, by its very nature, a very personal document, one that typifies *you* and nobody else. The way you tell your 'story' will tell the reader something about *you* between the lines.

Certain information, though, is clearly essential if your prospective employer is to ensure that you slot neatly into his requirements. This should come under five fairly distinctive headings as follows:

Personal

The first item to appear should be your name, preferably your full name although if there is a middle Christian name which you would rather people forget, make do with your commonly known first name followed by your surname.

If your sex is not clear from your first name, follow with the word 'Male' or 'Female'. If you believe it important, add your nationality, although this is not normally expected.

Your date of birth should follow next, and it is a good idea then to add your age merely to make it a little easier for the reader, saving him some mental arithmetic! Do not forget to change this when 'reprinting' (in practice, photo-copying) if a birthday intervenes.

Your married state should then appear, with details of children by sex and age. This is not essential information, and rarely relevant to the job in hand, but nevertheless is normally expected. Your new employer wants to feel he is getting to know you, even at this early stage.

Then put in your address in a proper Post Office manner, adding the necessary postcode. Before your telephone number, in brackets, add the dialling code.

There are two schools of thought as to whether details of your health should appear in a c.v. The first is the obvious one that you need to confirm your fitness, the second that, if nothing is said, this can be implied. Much will depend upon the type of position you are seeking. If good health is a special requirement, then reference to this helps the employer; otherwise such words as 'in good health' will more than suffice.

Qualifications

Whilst these need to be shown as comprehensively as possible, they should at the same time be angled towards your ultimate objective.

Your c.v., at its first airing, is likely to receive a scan only and it is up to you, through careful culling and highlighting, to make it worth a second glance. Periods of training, for instance, in a field which you now intend discarding in favour of another need to be skipped over lightly to prevent the reader homing in on that sector.

Similarly, some artistic licence is called for if there is a need to emphasize an area in which you are lightly experienced.

What you must never do, though, is to tell lies. Embroider, by all means but never fabricate. Your sins, as they say, will find you out, destroying for all time with that prospective employer any credibility which you might have had.

So carefully list your educational details, qualifications and specific periods of training but use the heavy hand here, the light one there to present an overall picture of the ideal candidate, the one whose c.v. will top the pile.

Schooling experience, as well as certificates, etc. gained, can play an important part in a c.v., more so the younger you are. So whether you captained the school football eleven or reached the grand rank of prefect, put it down.

Provide details of passes in GCE, CSE or, more latterly, GCSE, examinations, noting grades if you think that these will help.

College, polytechnic or university education details should appear next, amplified by any special attachments such as sandwich courses with industry or commerce. If you served an apprenticeship, provide details of your employer at the time coupled with any merit certificates obtained.

Courses, conferences, seminars and the like attended need adding to the list, particularly if they have especial reference to the job in hand. Similarly, if they have no obvious connection, they are best omitted!

Armed Forces experience may be appropriate although less so if the standard two years' National Service only was served. It may, however, pay you to refer to any special attachments or experience gained during this period, again only if job related.

This section, for many well qualified applicants, could quite easily take up a whole A4 sheet, but such verbiage is to be avoided. First, list all the qualifications, experience and training you can muster and then take a severe blue pencil and reduce the whole to no more than between a quarter and a third of such a sheet. In doing so you will create a tighter, more readable introduction to your document and, hopefully, encourage the reader to read on.

Experience

This is the meaty part; the part which many experienced c.v. readers tend to look at first of all. Faced with a pile of applicants' details perhaps several feet thick, a ruthless initial approach can be essential if the task is not to take several days. One method of achieving this is to skip the introductions and concentrate on the core of the c.v., i.e. the part which will tell the personnel officer whether or not you have the required experience for the job.

It is thus vital that you make this section both clear and interesting.

Whilst, as we have said above, it must be entirely truthful, there are different ways of saying the same thing. 'Some years spent in the drawing office' does not have the impact of 'Three years assisting Design Chief, notably with the production of new turbo aero engine', yet they could both be describing the same period of employment.

There could be occasions when some vagueness may be necessary to cloud a time in your career which you might feel had been of little benefit, but clearly these should be kept to a minimum. Clarity is the key; remember, you are dealing with a fast reader!

The general style of a c.v. will, of course, reflect *you* and, although there are no hard and fast rules in completing one, there do exist some more acceptable guidelines which you should follow.

One, for instance, is to use the impersonal sense and not the first person, i.e. 'I'. After a while, a succession of 'I's' begin to smack of self-importance. Adopting a factual tone, as you will see indicated in the examples below, allows you to appear less immodest and gives greater depth to your presentation.

This section, therefore, should incorporate a list in chronological order of your employers, commencing with the most recent and working backwards. It is normally sufficient to show merely the years between which you were employed on each occasion, the months being somewhat superfluous.

Following each heading should appear your job title or content, and a brief description of what this entailed. Bear in mind that, in this section especially, you are 'selling' yourself and therefore bring out clearly any successes or achievements during each period of employment. Studying the examples will give you the flavour of what you must achieve here. Job titles should immediately conjure up the type of work with which you were involved and, if your company made use of rather lengthy, but meaningless, titles then change them when constructing your c.v. This practice is perfectly acceptable, as long as you do not meaningfully exaggerate. 'B Section Production Responsibility' is better translated into, say, 'Production Controller' providing this is what it really meant!

If your job was not blessed with a title, as is still the case in large sections of industry in particular, then make one up which neatly fits what you were doing. If you looked after part of, say, a lending manager's portfolio in a bank which incorporated other duties of a fairly general nature, using the title 'Lending Manager's Assistant' could be perfectly justifiable if this role predominated. Remember, however, that references may be sought and anything contained in your c.v. which later proves to be untrue will naturally be held against you.

Each description needs to be as specific as possible; waffle will not get you anywhere and you will probably end up on the scrapheap! Use data where appropriate but make this positive, generally in round terms clearly understood by the recruiter.

If you were responsible for increasing sales, then say so but make it quite clear by how much, such as 'During two year spell, raised turnover from £2 million to £3 million'.

This part of your c.v. should also list any professional or honorary appointments of note, providing they relate directly to your fields of experience. Membership of the Bar Committee of your cricket club hardly qualifies for a mention, but Secretary of the local branch of your professional institution certainly would. Be careful, though, not to over-emphasize outside occupations or a prospective employer might well wonder whether you have sufficient time for work!

On the other hand, most employers do expect their workers to have some intelligent outside activity and, indeed, printed application forms normally reserve a space for these to be listed.

Remuneration

If there is one thing that the British are coy about, it is how much they earn. Party talk will invariably centre around where you live, what you do and which school your children attend — but NEVER how much you are paid. If someone boasts about his level of earnings, then almost certainly he is exaggerating. He is probably adding bonuses, 'perks' and a little more, and calling the end result a 'salary.'

It is certainly not essential to make reference within a c.v. to your salary. But if you have set your sights on a certain level of earnings, and are not prepared to take anything which pays less, then you have nothing to lose by adding a paragraph explaining your requirements. Be specific. Say something like 'Basic salary indicator required £25,000 plus usual benefits' rather than 'Package sought in the region of £25,000 to £30,000'. The latter, in any event, is more likely to attract the lower level rather than the higher.

There is certainly no need to quote current or past salaries, although be prepared to talk about these at interview. This is discussed in Chapter 9.

Resumé

It is unlikely that you will have time — or patience! — to prepare a c.v.

for each job application. We will assume, therefore, that you are aiming to produce a general document that will suffice for each prospective employer.

What you can quite cleverly do, though, is to attach a resumé which can be written with a specific job in mind. This will be especially useful if you are aiming at a career change, because you will need to make it quite plain to the reader that, despite the background as evidenced by your c.v., you believe that you have much to offer in his field.

A resumé can be used to achieve two ends. First, it brings out and highlights relevant c.v. content whilst, secondly, it reinforces your suitability for the job in hand. Your target is to convince your next employer that he needs you and the resumé provides this opportunity. It also makes possible a short covering letter which most personnel managers welcome.

The resumé should consist of no more than half an A4 sheet and, ideally, only three or four paragraphs. If your c.v. already runs to two full A4 sheets, then do not staple these together until you have completed the relevant resumé which can then be added behind the other two before stapling. If you have sufficient room on your second c.v. sheet to add a resumé, then type up page two on each occasion unless you are fully confident that your lining up will not give away the fact that it is merely an addition to a standard document.

If you are applying for a senior position overseas, then a dossier will come in handy. This is no more than an expanded c.v., usually accompanied by a photograph of yourself, contained within a smart binder. This is invariably a requirement abroad, especially within Europe or the United States of America.

Label the cover neatly, possibly using transfers such as Letraset, and include:

- Full personal details, including nationality and expertise in languages;
- Detailed qualifications;
- Experience;
- Details of any publications for which you have been responsible; and
- References.

You will need two or three copies at least and these should normally be sent by Registered Post where possible.

. . . And Finally

Remember to keep your covering letter brief and to the point.

References need not form part of your c.v., although a note of where these might be obtained can be added if you wish. Out of courtesy, prime any potential referees first and try and provide them with reasons why you are seeking a change. Do not attempt to influence them in what they say; this will only appear conceited and could result in their being less immodest about you than they would otherwise have been!

Special problems which can arise in completing a c.v. are as follows:

Several years in only one employment: in this case, provide details of each position held and in your covering letter try to justify your reasons for now wanting to make a change. Do not make the mistake of stretching out these details in the c.v. just for the sake of it;

Currently self-employed: treat this as if you were working for someone else, except for the job title, and therefore give details of the nature of the job and any achievements, etc. Your covering letter will need to explain why you now wish to liquidate your business and seek re-employment;

Periods of unemployment: unless these span more than a 12 month period, they can probably be overlooked. A longer spell, however, will have to be accounted for in your chronological order but this could work in your favour if, for instance, you undertook any training whilst unemployed. Course details may be entered as an alternative, leaving the interview for a fuller explanation. Another possibility might be your preference for a particular type of job for which there were no vacancies for some time.

Fluency in any language should obviously be quoted in your c.v., indicating whether you are truly 'fluent' or merely 'passable'.

Finally, provide details of any publications for which you have been responsible, either in a sole capacity or working with others. Notable articles may also be relevant, as might your working on patents.

An Example C.V.

Personal

John Brown
10 Abberton Crescent,
Coventry,
Warwickshire.

Telephone: (0203)-741693

Born 30th June, 1947; age 42

Married, four children: Stephen 19; Nicola 13; Louise 12; Michelle 3.

Health: good.

Qualifications

Bablake Grammar School: 7 GCE O Levels
Associate: Institute of Bankers
Associate: Institute of Chartered Secretaries

Career details

1984 – date:	Occupax Ltd: Company Secretary Responsible for all statutory duties of both parent company and four subsidiaries.
1978–1984:	Registrex Ltd: Assistant Company Secretary
1963–1978:	Barcloyds Bank Ltd. Various positions, including: Manager's Assistant Office Manager Assistant Branch Manager

(Details of each of these positions should be included)

Remuneration

Minimum salary of £27,500 sought, with usual benefits and Company car.

Leisure pursuits

Cricket; Sunday League county player.
Treasurer, local branch Institute of Chartered Secretaries.

This is a skeleton approach only, intended to give you a flavour of how a c.v. should look. In practice, the more important points would be amplified and, in particular, those relating to the new position you seek highlighted.

Now that you have your c.v. prepared, let us get down to replying to those job advertisements . . .

CHAPTER 8

Replying to Advertisements

The very first 'contact' you make with your hoped-for employer will normally be through the medium of your covering letter. There is thus little to be gained from producing a perfect c.v. attached to a less than perfect letter. Both documents must receive your detailed attention.

To the receiver you are still goods on the shelf, as yet unpurchased. The can has still to be opened; what is being scrutinised at this stage is the label.

Most of us abhor writing letters; it is a task which invariably gets pushed to the bottom of anyone's list. But these letters are the most important you will ever write in your life; they are, in fact, likely to change your life. Land the right — better — job and the 'dividends' will come pouring in for years to come.

This part of your job hunting exercise, therefore, is, in some respects, the most vital. Approach it methodically and efficiently. Method here is most important and lack of it may cost you the one job which you would really have coveted; lack of efficiency may land you in an awful mess, to the extent perhaps of being granted an interview without knowing what you have told the recruiter so far.

It is not a bad idea to set yourself some targets. These may be based either upon the number of job applications you set yourself, or the time you are prepared to allocate to the task. Ideally, they will encompass both disciplines although in the early days some flexibility will be needed until you adjust to the job in hand and discover how long the job searching takes.

It will comprise four functions as follows:

1. Identifying which newspapers and magazines you should be studying;
2. Seeking out those positions for which you consider yourself suitable;
3. Getting down to the business of writing; and
4. Maintaining clear records of what you have done.

Let us take them in order.

First, buy (or browse — possibly in your local library) copies of every major national newspaper for a week. You will then discover which might in future be ignored and those you will have to continue buying. By spanning a full week you will also find out those newspapers which run special job advertisement features on specific days. The *Daily Telegraph* and The *Financial Times* are two cases in point; you will not need to buy copies every day!

Order from your newsagent any local newspapers produced on either a city or county basis. Finally, make arrangements to see regularly — and as near to publication date as possible — those trade magazines likely to feature vacancies of interest to you.

With your criteria list by your side, scan the job advertisements carefully and cut these out, immediately marking them with their source and date. If one should appear on the reverse of another, use a blank sheet for one marked 'See reverse of . . .' and use this as your filing record.

This only leaves you to write an appropriate letter and maintain a record of what you have done. Methods of keeping these records were discussed in Chapter 4 and you may care to look back on these as a refresher.

Targets likely to be achieved are, say, writing three letters a day if you are already employed, increasing this to double this number if you are currently unemployed. The number may, of course, be determined by vacancies available and, clearly, letters should not be despatched merely to meet targets. Nor should you, at this early stage, vary your criteria by very much although, if the going gets tough, this will have to be reviewed.

Cost has already been mentioned in Chapter 4 and the actual writing of the letters is only one item in what could be a not insignificant bill. Ignoring notepaper and envelopes, postage stamps alone will set you back around £12 a month utilising the above 'employed' target, and twice this if you use the higher figure. First class post, though, is essential unless a closing date some time ahead is quoted in the advertisement.

Whilst target figures have been suggested, your ideal must be to reply to every advertisement which comes within your criteria. Miss just one and it might have been the one for you; unfortunately, you will never know!

If you are in the fortunate position of having numerous advertisements to which you can sensibly reply, then some culling may be advisable. Alternatively, you can set your own sights a little higher!

What to Look Out for

Advertisements for jobs come in all shapes and sizes, from three lines in the local classified section to whole pages in the national dailies. After a while — (although hopefully it will not be for too long!) — you will become an expert in scanning newspaper and journal pages for jobs which appeal.

Do not discard advertisements too quickly. At the beginning let the details soak in to test whether or not they meet your basic criteria; some which, at first, may not have any appeal, might, on second sighting, be worth a try.

You are looking out for certain basic details which generally appear in all job advertisements. Categorise them as follows:

Job Title

This might be quite specific, such as 'Group Legal Manager' or more general such as 'Sales Executive'. The former is quite clear in its meaning, although more delving is necessary to find out the size of the group, whilst the latter could mean just about anything, from door-to-door knocking drumming up business for encyclopaedias to a much more high-powered position.

Artistic licence is rife in setting job titles and many a would-be hopeful 'Trainee Manager' especially, for instance, in the retailing sector, has left after only a few weeks when realisation dawned that all that was wanted was a sales assistant. Just as practice makes perfect, so you will become an expert in spotting the real meanings behind the fancy phrases when you have read your first 200 job advertisements!

Job Description

This can be equally misleading, although generally it should guide you as to whether or not it meets your horizons.

The better advertisements do tend to provide a fairly clear description of what you will be expected to do and, quite often, to whom you will report. This latter point often provides a clue as to the level of the position much better than the actual title can do. Let us take 'Group Legal Manager' again. The advertisement goes on to say that you will report directly to the Group Secretary so that obviously he will be your immediate superior. It might have indicated reporting directly to the Board, in which case the position would carry a much greater degree of authority, not necessarily, of course, reflected in the remuneration package.

Read the job description carefully and several times over before adding it to your list of enquiries. Whilst there is by no means a demand at this stage of your meeting all that it calls for, you will certainly have to prove your worthiness in a majority of items.

Experience Required

This should not prove too difficult to identify although, once again, do not be deterred by the fact that you may not meet every requirement quoted.

Much will depend on the wording used. Obviously if the advertisement states 'Must have had a minimum of five years working in the insurance industry', it would be silly to apply if your experience amounted to only 12 months. On the other hand, 'A good academic background combined with technical skills and the ability to develop within a challenging environment is required' might fit just about anybody with solid experience and a silvery tongue!

Many advertisements today do not call for specific experience. More frequently sought is a candidate who 'must be able to communicate clearly and who has the ability to assume responsibility quickly', etc. Your powers of persuasion will surely overcome this apparent obstacle!

Qualifications

These generally come a little more cut and dried and if an 'MA (Hons.)' is sought, you will only be wasting your own time if you have anything less, although rare exceptions can still apply if you meet every other requirement called for.

You will, presumably, already have set your horizons based upon experience and qualifications and should not, therefore, be disappointed too often by what employers are seeking. On the other hand, if it becomes lucidly clear after a while that you are just not going to get past the post with the qualifications you already hold, then return to Chapter 5 for another look at 'Retraining for a Fresh Start'.

Sector and Company

Whilst the latter may not always be clear from the advertisement, the former should generally be so. Your criteria will already have aimed you at certain sectors of the job market but keep an open mind at this stage. Many highly successful business people have switched sectors at important stages of their careers simply because the new challenge appealed.

Most major companies tend to use agencies for their placements and, in their advertisements, the client is not named. This is probably less important than you might at first imagine for it enables this component of the formula not to cloud your judgement. Should you by any chance apply for another job with your present employer without appreciating the fact, the agency will seek your permission before communicating your interest.

Location

This will generally be shown, if not the town then almost certainly the area, i.e. 'the South East', 'north of England' and so on.

You will already have mapped out your geographical parameters so it will not take you too long to decide whether or not to discard the particular advertisement. What might be less clear is the area in which you will be expected to operate and only an interview can clarify this. Make sure you ask the question!

Age Limit

Probably the most difficult of all barriers if the employer is being sticky about the age of the person he is looking for. He is, naturally, quite entitled to lay down the ground rules and you would be unwise to attempt to change them too dramatically.

There will be occasions when you feel it might be worth a try. But to write 'I meet all your requirements, although I am aged 54' when his advertisement has stated an age band of '30 to 40' is pushing your luck just a little too far! Nevertheless, do not be afraid of going outside stated demands if you feel your case is a strong one; it will only cost you another stamp.

Remuneration Package

This is one of those areas where only experience is going to give you a clearer understanding of the many different ways in which salaries and associated 'perks' are quoted in job advertisements. '£25,000 per annum plus car' is quite clear. More than likely, however, you will see such statements as 'For the right person we are prepared to pay the right price', or 'The successful candidate will receive a competitive remuneration package and the opportunity to substantially develop his future expectations'.

This is where you must do your homework and, through diligent research and much reading of vacancy notices, have a clear idea of, first, what you are worth and, secondly, what any particular prospective employer might pay you. The answers, which inevitably will coincide at some point, will probably lie somewhere within a band with, on average, perhaps £5,000 or so between the two extremes. It is probably a good idea to segregate in your own mind salary expectation, and perquisites.

Having settled on a band for the former, it will help to clarify in your own mind your level of demand for the latter. If you finish up with the lower end of the expected band, then clearly the need for a company car, travelling expenses or whatever else will supplement this becomes greater; at the top of the band, you may decide to forego some of these 'demands'.

What to Say

Whatever you say in your covering letter, present it neatly. This is your first contact and, in the absence of being there in person, your letter has to sell *you*. It should be on good quality paper and normally typewritten; only if the advertisement calls for a handwritten reply should this rule be broken. It goes without saying that it must not contain any errors. Wherever possible, ask a friend to read it through before you despatch it; if the writer's eye and the reader's are the same, mistakes can slip through.

Have photographs ready should these be called for, although this is less usual these days. No stamped addressed envelope need be included.

Before putting pen to paper, re-read the advertisement to which you are about to reply. Is there anything which you had not spotted the first time? Are you quite certain this is the job for you?

Having convinced yourself that this is the case, put together a sharp, crisp letter that does not merely repeat much of what is contained in your c.v., to which you will attach it, but which draws out the salient arguments in your case. Say why you are the person for the job, refer to any special aptitudes you possess and finish off by adding any period of notice which you may have to give to your present employer along with your availability for interviews should this be restricted.

Address the letter precisely to the intended recipient and add any references which are called for. If your present rate of remuneration is sought, then an indication of this must be provided; if you do not answer this question, then almost certainly your application will go straight into the bin.

Reasons for having already left your most recent employment, if this is the case, need to be thought out carefully. Remember that enquiries may be made and the two stories should tally, at least in general content. If there was a clash of personalities, it is probably better to say so than to fictionalise; if you get to the interview, you will at least be able to put your case personally.

The last point to remember about your covering letters is that, if you fail consistently to obtain interviews, they will require a rethink. Perhaps they are too long or too short? Seek advice and listen carefully to constructive criticism.

A Sample Covering Letter

20 The Grove
Stratford on Avon,
Warwickshire.

Date

Your Reference:

The Personnel Manager,
Ridings Cartons Ltd.,
Leamington Spa,
Warwickshire.

Dear Sir,

I have been particularly attracted by your advertisement for a Sales Manager in today's 'Times'.

You will see from my attached c.v. that I have spent some years working in industry although mainly in a technical capacity. My present employers recently asked me to become responsible for the sales function additionally and I have found this very rewarding.

I would now welcome a move to a dedicated sales function which my employers are unable to provide. I believe that your customers would have greater confidence in placing orders with someone with a technical background.

My notice period is four weeks. I look forward to hearing from you.

Yours faithfully,
P. ADAMS

Providing References

One of the most difficult decisions facing you is who you should ask to act as your referees; usually two are required. These can be former (or, indeed, present) colleagues or friends; relatives are best avoided. Whoever you approach they themselves should have certain qualities:

- They should know you very well;
- They should be sympathetic to your cause;
- They should, if at all possible, hold some senior position or at least carry enough authority to sway others towards their opinion of you; and
- Be conversant with the type of job you have in mind.

They are best approached quite early on in your campaign. Do not be offended if they ask to be excused; they may have very good personal reasons for not wishing to write you what is virtually a 'blank cheque' in the recruitment sense. Some people find it difficult to write character references for others, however well they may know them, and this must be respected.

If you have a wide circle of friends and acquaintances, choose carefully. Study the above factors and, in particular, pick someone who is likely to speak well of you in a specific rather than a general manner. 'I have known X for some years and have never heard anything bad about him' is quite useless; your reference should point to particular aspects of excellence and, beyond being a character reference, should ideally refer to your achievements — and, possibly, aspirations.

If your referee is a Member of Parliament, a bank manager, a head teacher, or someone hopefully equally above reproach, so much the better. If you are 'well connected', take advantage of it carefully to avoid cries of nepotism. One Asian student, here on a degree course, gave, as 'occupation of father' a Crown Prince and provided the king as a referee!

Keep your referees fully in the picture. Grab an opportunity — or make one if necessary — to explain in some detail your reasons for seeking a better job and ask if he or she feels able to provide you with a suitable reference. Guide your potential referee by all means to the areas you feel would most sensibly be covered, but do not tell him what to say! Accept the fact, incidentally, that you will never see a copy of his letter; most referees prefer to remain discreet about what they have actually said.

Completing Application Forms

It is quite frustrating, having given a great deal of thought to the compilation of your c.v., to receive a reply from a prospective employer asking you to complete one of his standard application forms. The temptation is to throw it in the bin and write back referring to the fact that you have already forwarded your c.v. Do not do this! This is an absolutely fatal move and will certainly eliminate you from the chase.

Every employer has a differing method of maintaining employee records and you must respect this fact. Although in completing his form you will be repeating much of what is already contained in your c.v., you will, nevertheless, be stating it in a manner familiar to him.

The first thing you should do, upon receiving an application form, is to photocopy it and complete the copied version. Only when you feel that you have got it right should you transfer the information to the original form. Nothing looks worse than corrections at this early stage of your 'acquaintance' and many of these forms are not all that straightforward to complete.

In general they are probably best handwritten, in capitals if you prefer, simply because their boxed approach is not very conducive to the typewriter.

Keep your answers short and concise and certainly do not attempt to expand beyond the boxes. Angle your facts toward the job in hand but ensure that what you say does not clash with anything contained in your c.v.!

Do answer every question, although some may appear irrelevant. Most job application forms tend to be general rather than specific and some of the information called for may not, therefore, apply to your case; nevertheless, do your best to provide the information requested.

There is frequently a large blank space at the end of the form to enable you to add anything of your own. It is generally better to complete rather than to ignore this section to allow you to distinguish yourself from other candidates. Give it, therefore, a great deal of thought.

Provide the reader of the form with tangible reasons why he should keep *you* on his list whilst weeding out others. Outline your strengths and keep these to aspects directly related to the job for which you are applying. This is the time for the hard sell.

You should, therefore, know a great deal about the company you hope to join. If necessary, do your homework at the library and if you can pick up on something in which they specialise and for which you consider yourself eminently suitable, link these together in a mouth-watering manner. There is no need to be humble, although similarly bragging is out of the question; somewhere in between you have to whet the appetite of the recruiter.

If black ink is called for in completing the form, use it. The very good reason for this is ease of copying. Why anger the reader by using anything else?

Before despatching the form, re-read it and ensure there are no blanks, spelling mistakes or grammatical errors. Sign and date it as called for and attach your brief covering letter and any other documentation requested. Ensure that any references to be marked on your envelope are not missed; doing so may delay the receipt of your form by the correct person, especially if an agency is being used.

Apart from sorting out application forms from unsuitable candidates, recruiters have two other methods available to them of 'testing' suitability long before an interview. One of these is a psychological testing form and the other the use of handwriting techniques or graphology.

The psychological form is usually quite easy to spot, since numbers used to 'weight' candidates' answers appear down the side, alongside each question. The questions themselves often appear quite irrelevant, such as 'State your childhood ambitions' or 'What would you do in the event of . . .?' but, if you remain serious about applying for that particular job, grit your teeth and sharpen your pencil.

Generally, truth will out in this type of test and you will be wasting your time if you try to cheat. Questions in one section of the form generally link with questions asked later, but this will not be obvious at the time. Trying to state what you believe you should be stating rather than what might be the absolute truth is child's play in a psychologist's hands. He will make mincemeat of you — but you will never know it; you will simply not hear from the firm again!

If you are asked to complete a form, or part of it, in your own handwriting, you must, of course, do so. This may not indicate a hidden graphology check but, on the other hand, it may — either way the choice is not yours.

Speculative Applications

These give rise to two schools of thought. There are those who consider them a complete waste of time, energy and cost; others will point to instances where better jobs have been gained by adopting such a method. In the author's view there is nothing to be lost by trying this approach if only to test the water; certainly if the job advertisements you are seeking have tended to dry up, then fill in with this method.

It does, however, call for positive treatment. Just despatching standard letters to any company name that comes to mind will only get you a bad name.

The Field Marshal's approach is the only one. Think of your campaign as a war, and go all out to win.

Draw up a list of, say, half a dozen companies appropriate to your search. They may be of any size but clearly the larger concerns will have the greater job opportunities. Research them thoroughly and make sure you know the job description you are seeking.

Rather than pen your introductory letter to no one in particular, it is important to make it land on the right desk immediately. A telephone call will usually elicit from a helpful telephonist the name of the personnel manager; have a pen ready and ask his initials and precise title. Then address your letter appropriately and begin it 'Dear Mr. . . .'

Letters should be brief, but tantalising. Your only objective — bearing in mind that a vacancy does not actually exist — is to attract the eye of the personnel manager and encourage him into thinking that you could be a potential candidate should an appropriate job become vacant. If you can do this, you have, of course, made his job that much easier; you may have saved him advertising cost and a great deal of time. He may even be eternally grateful!

All that your letter can contain is a reference to your availability and a request that you be borne in mind; your c.v., which you will attach, must do the rest.

You should, at least, obtain a response; lack of it may indicate a company for whom you would rather not work. The best that you can normally hope for at this stage is to be placed on a waiting list with possibly some priority when a job occurs.

Your letter should run along the following lines:

Dear Mr. Prentice,

I am currently seeking an improved position in the area of retail management and write in the hope that you may have a vacancy.

For the past seven years I have managed a department of Riders Stores and during that time departmental profitability has risen by 230%. I would now like to manage something larger and feel that many opportunities must exist within your expanding organisation.

I am attaching a detailed c.v. and would very much welcome an interview if you feel my qualifications and experience appropriate. I would need to give one month's notice at Riders.

I look forward to hearing from you.

Yours sincerely,

Do not expect magic from this source. But by gaining yourself a place as first reserve you will have done yourself no harm.

Using the Telephone

This is not the generally accepted medium for job searchers, but it can have its uses.

If, for instance, you live in an area of high employment, with subsequent rapid turnover of employees, using the telephone may save you a great deal of time.

You are after only one thing. You need to know whether or not the company you are telephoning would welcome a job application from you at the present time. To be certain of this, you must normally speak to the decision maker, and that might be the personnel manager or even the managing director.

Start with a call to the switchboard. Ask for the personnel manager's name and follow this with a request to speak to him. If you get beyond the switchboard, almost certainly the next voice you hear will be that of a secretary and you must again make your request. She will probably ask you the reason for the call and at this stage you must be honest; simply say that you wish to enquire whether any vacancies might exist in a particular field. Invariably she will give you an answer herself and that answer will, again invariably, be in the negative. Persist, but only gently; anything other than perfect manners and a calm voice will lose you your case. If you are told quite positively that Mr. X does not take that type of call, accept it and say that you will write in instead. If you are lucky enough to be put through, then you are on your own.

Apologise briefly for troubling him, say who you are and your current position and follow this by the fact that you are seeking a better job in a specific field. The rest you will have to play by ear!

Do not ring at 5.20 p.m. on a Friday. Early morning is probably the best time.

A Few Golden Rules

There is really only one (Write, write, write), but keep your eye on the following to be really successful:

- Adopt a positive, strategical approach to replying to job advertisements;
- Set yourself targets and review these weekly;
- Maintain thorough records of everything you do;
- Re-read the advertisement before you complete your letter;
- Re-read your letter before you seal the envelope.

You might also like to have a note of what one head hunter tells employers in an effort to whittle down a large number of replies. Any one of the following qualifies for the bin:

- Mis-spelling of the company's name or address;
- Ignoring the instructions on how to reply;
- Omitting your address or a legible version of your name;
- Sending a poorly photocopied standard letter;
- Demanding more information about the job without offering anything more about yourself;
- Sending a c.v. of more than two pages;
- Making no effort to show how you meet the various requirements specified by the advertisement;
- Failing to quote a reference or the job title, or to say where you saw the advertisement;
- Avoiding mention of your age or present salary.

So be warned! Now let us get you through the interview successfully . . .

CHAPTER 9

Handling Interviews Successfully

Before you can get a better job, of course, you must first of all get an interview. Your first objective, therefore, has been to reach this critical point in your campaign and, hopefully, your c.v. and accompanying letter will have achieved this for you.

It is a very comforting, and indeed exciting, moment when you receive your first invitation to an interview. This invitation may reach you in one of two forms, either by letter or by telephone. Very often employers are anxious to fill posts and they can save themselves time by making telephoned arrangements with applicants. In writing to you, the suggested interview timing may prove inconvenient or impossible — although you should make yourself fairly readily available — and a rearranged date will only postpone matters further.

Once you have despatched your first application, therefore, be prepared to take a telephone call asking you to an interview. Warn your family should one of them answer the telephone in your absence and make sure the answering is done in a professional manner. Whenever answering the telephone, it is advisable to say: 'Hello, this is . . . Can I help you?' Have your diary handy and be certain that the day and time suggested are convenient.

This is your first 'contact' with what could be your next employer. Do not let yourself down.

If the offer of an interview comes through the post, reply immediately and preferably by telephone to confirm your acceptance. You will probably only get as far as the Personnel Manager's secretary, but your only job at this stage is to say that you will be there at the appointed time. Ask if written confirmation is needed and follow whatever other instructions are given to you.

Know Your Interviewer

How, you may ask, can you possibly know anything about the man or woman who is going to interview you? This is not as ridiculous as it at first sounds, because by diligent research on the company you are about to visit, you may well along the way learn quite a lot about its employees and the way in which it is run.

You have quite a job ahead of you but almost certainly it will pay

handsome dividends — in the ultimate, the offer of a better job!
You must now find out:

- Precisely what the company does;
- Details of its products or services;
- Where it is located in terms of branch or regional structures, and whether it is represented abroad;
- Its size and profitability;
- Its reputation and any special features; and
- Any up-to-date aspects which could have a bearing upon the job for which you have applied.

Depending upon the size of the company, none of this is as difficult to discover as you might imagine. Go back to Chapter 4 for a list of research material with which you should by now have become familiar and search specifically against the company you are about to visit.

You may, of course, have already carried out this exercise as advised earlier, although if you are sending out job applications by the dozen it may have proved somewhat daunting!

Trade journals (many of which are available in major libraries) can be a fruitful source of information here as can your local Chamber of Commerce, especially if your target company is relatively small. Your bank may be able to obtain up-to-date accounting information if your library is unable to help.

Tackle friends and relations again; it is surprising just how much people know about local industry. If you know someone who already works there, your battle is half won and almost certainly he will be able to tell you something about the person who is likely to interview you.

Brochures, if these are produced, will reveal a great deal about the business; so will a visit if it is readily accessible, such as a shop, or otherwise open to the public. If the company is large enough it will probably have its own public relations department and they will normally be quite willing to help you in your research if you explain your reasons. If the company exhibits at a trade fair or exhibition, pop along if you can to find out a little more about it.

And do not forget to re-read the advertisement to which you originally replied. Sometimes this can be quite revealing.

Adopt a Strategy

Well before the day of the interview make notes of the points you feel should be covered and what questions you want to ask. List these in order of priority and study the list until you feel that you know it fairly well. Try to memorise the most salient features and have a reasonably clear idea of how you believe the interview should run. It is not, in practice, likely to run in anything like the order you expected, but you will at least have adopted a common sense strategy and, with luck, will recall its most important features.

Most professional interviewers will put you at your ease and you should not feel tense or nervous, but should you meet someone less structured, this should be turned in your favour and you will have an opportunity of 'conducting' the interview along the lines of your adopted strategy.

Most interviews get off to a fairly light-hearted start, with the day's weather and perhaps details of your journey being discussed. After perhaps three or four minutes, however, you should note a perceptible change in the interviewer's stance and this is where the interview proper really begins. Grab the opportunity during those opening minutes to make yourself fully comfortable, to put on a pleasant countenance, and generally to relax. Then, when the real questioning begins, you will be prepared and exude the sort of confidence that the recruiter is looking for.

If he appears by nature an aggressive individual, counter this with tolerance and under no circumstances try to match his aggression. If you are the sort of person who is easily aroused, you will have to learn to temper this in an interview situation; an argumentative nature will only lose you points.

Avoid talking too much but, equally, do not give simple 'Yes' and 'No' answers. Expand a little upon each question raised, just enough to arouse the interviewer's interest but without boring him. If, by providing a detailed answer, you can inject something particularly interesting into the interview, then by all means do so. Expanding upon some aspect of your c.v., for instance, may offer an opportunity of upgrading the importance of that particular point in the interviewer's mind and put you higher up his mental list of 'possibles'.

Avoid merely repeating what has already been said in your c.v. What the interviewer is looking for is a little meat on that particular bone and, especially, something relevant to the job in hand. Time is generally against you in an interview and it is vital that you distinguish the important from the less important and highlight only the former.

Do not boast openly, but you are allowed to move a few bushels to reveal some light. Having done so, however, keep your achievements brief; the interviewer will let you know if he would welcome some expansion of them.

Never run down former employers. Have a readily acceptable reason (which may differ in some small degree from the truth!) as to why you left each job detailed in your c.v. By all means speak of personality clashes which are quite acceptable in today's business world — but do not have too many of them!

Finally, your upfront strategy should include being prepared with details of suitable referees and, if it is appropriate to the job, prepare to take with you examples of your work such as designs, photographs or awards gained.

Present Yourself Properly

Timing is all important. You will have been provided with a time and a place and it is up to you to be there. Starting your interview with an excuse as to why you are late is hardly going to put you in the best light as a potential employee.

Be absolutely sure, therefore, how long you need to make available for the journey. If you are going to have to rely upon public transport, check the times and catch one bus or train earlier than is really necessary; if parking has to be found, make certain you know where to find this. You may have been sent a map to help you locate your destination; if the area is strange to you, check it out beforehand, for such maps are often not to scale and distances can be misleading.

Preferably, arrive quarter of an hour or so earlier than the appointed time. Then take a leisurely stroll, gathering your thoughts on the way, for five minutes in one direction, returning via the same route, leaving you just five minutes to announce yourself to reception.

If you are kept waiting by the interviewer, do not let this affect your polished performance. Remember, he is a busy man and has more excuses than you have for running a little over his schedule. He should, naturally, apologise, but if this is missing, simply ignore it.

What you should wear must remain a personal choice, but do not overdress. For either sex, a suit cannot be beaten for most job interviews, although something a little more casual may certainly be in order on a few occasions. Most importantly, wear something in which you feel comfortable, although jeans are certainly out.

Whatever the clothes, they should be clean and well-pressed and your hair at its smartest. A faint aroma of perfume, or body deodorant, will not go amiss, but avoid overdoing it. Obviously your breath must not smell of alcohol, so however tempting it might be to have a strong drink beforehand, avoid it like the plague.

If you are taking papers along with you, they are best carried in a slim briefcase; anything ostentatious will not count in your favour.

Smile as you enter the room and be ready with a firm handshake; make the first move if necessary. Wait to be told to sit down, although if the offer is not forthcoming, merely let a moment elapse before doing so. Do not smoke unless specifically offered a cigarette and then, of course, only if you are a smoker! Look straight at the interviewer.

Be Yourself

You are dealing with a professional and he will see through any 'disguise' you care to adopt, whether it is a change of accent, an emblazoned story or even an intentional blanking out of a period of your life.

Adopted accents are particularly prone to slippage under stress and should therefore be avoided. Do not be ashamed if you own an especially strong regional accent; since the adoption many years ago by the BBC of 'dialect broadcasters', these are quite acceptable in most job situations.

Your aim must be to be yourself; do not apologise for anything and this will include previous positions of which you may not be particularly proud or reasons for leaving them. If you are uncertain of the answer to a question, admit it rather than waffling; you will only be caught out later.

Never argue with the interviewer, although equally never be afraid to express a view as long as you can fully justify it. Do not get into a political argument, however strong your views.

Make certain that you are answering the question asked. Many interviewees make the mistake of picking up on a particular point referred to in a question and wandering down a verbal avenue without actually providing the answer. Pause if necessary before responding; do not feel that quickfire answers are called for. The interviewer would rather have a well-considered opinion than a rushed view.

Be positive in your answering. Every recruiter is looking for a well-rounded, confident individual to employ and your job is to make him feel at home with you on board. He will often have to justify taking you on to a superior or divisional colleague and if he is able to point to apparent qualities of leadership and confidence, these may overcome any shortcomings in your experience and/or qualifications.

Your strengths and weaknesses are likely to emerge during interviewing and it is up to you to identify when they do so, subsequently playing on strengths and sliding over weaknesses. At the same time the recruiter is likely to be seeking a reversal of this tactic, highlighting especially any areas where he may feel you are unsuitable for the job. Do not overplay your card in this area; your preparatory work should have covered such eventualities and this is the time to offer your reasons why you should be able to overcome any deficiencies. State them clearly and briefly — and then shut up!

Never swear and under no circumstances become emotional. This does not prevent you from showing enthusiasm or concern if this is genuinely felt, but, having expressed a view, return your mind and mouth to the calm mode and await the next question.

If you feel that your voice is going to let you down, do not despair! There are agencies which can assist you, such as Voiceworks, of London, which offers a number of exercises and tips to people wishing to get the most out of their voices, including:

- Control your breath at all times. Breathe low in the body and let the abdominal muscles out as you breathe in, contracting them as you breathe out.

- Breathe out if you feel yourself under stress.
- Sit up straight when facing an interviewer.
- As already suggested, use pauses to gain confidence.
- Listen intently and show that you are being receptive by nodding occasionally or saying, for instance, 'I agree'.
- Sing to yourself, aiming at extending your pitch range!

Questions You May Be Faced with

An interview is all about questions — or is it? It is really, of course, much more about answers, and not only what they contain but how they are presented.

The interviewer's assessment of you will build up gradually over a period, although one probably lasting no more than, say, half an hour. Remember that you have already impressed him with your c.v. and covering letter, or you would not be sitting where you are, but great care is now needed not to destroy that favourable impression upon face-to-face contact. The manner in which you provide answers, therefore, is just as important as what they contain, yet with thorough preparation you can do much more about the manner than the content.

The secret is to guess what the questions might be before you present yourself at the interview; not quite as difficult as you might imagine, for most interviews fall into a pattern. Questioners will ask you about (a) yourself (b) your background and qualifications and (c) your likely suitability for the job in question.

Be prepared, therefore, for personal questions such as:

Did you enjoy working at . . .?
What made you leave?
What precise responsibilities were you given?
Was the job demanding?
What did you achieve during your time there?

And so on. Consider answers to each of these points and how you would tackle them; jot down brief details to make them stick more easily in the memory. Then prepare for more difficult questions like:

What makes you think you are suitable for this job?
What do you know about this company? (Here your research should stand you in good stead.)
How would you tackle our problems?
Do you consider you have any weaknesses? (Never admit to these!)

And, finally, prepare as far as you are able for tough ones such as:

What do you consider the most important department in the company?
How would you go about making colleagues redundant?

Tell me how you would sell our product.

Why do you read so-and-so newspaper?

How would you tackle a clash of personalities between departmental heads?

It is, of course, impossible to gauge precisely what questions you might be asked upfront, but at least prepare for all of the above and, whilst you are doing so, throw a few of your own in for good measure.

We have covered general questions only. Naturally, depending upon what type of job it is for which you are applying, expect technical questioning in addition.

Whatever the question, handle it as confidently as you are able. Do not lie, for it will quickly show; better to be honest than to be shown up. No interviewer will welcome you wasting his time in lengthy, but obviously incorrect, answers to technical questions.

Some Questions to Ask

Many of the queries buzzing around in your head should, hopefully, have answered themselves as the interview progresses. Have a check-list ready, although do not make a point of running down every question; use it as a guide only but do not be afraid of putting it on the desk before you. If you do this, make certain that it is neatly presented and does not contain specific references to any contentious questions; it is surprising how many recruiters can read upside down!

Your own questions should centre around your suitability for the job rather than the job's suitability for you. Show the personnel officer that you really care about working for his company by asking, for instance:

Do you believe that my experience would prove beneficial in this post?

Is there some way in which I might learn a little more about your company?

Would any training periods be of benefit before taking up this position?

Does the job entail any special difficulties which I should know about?

For whom would I be working, and what precisely is the chain of command?

Are there opportunities for further promotion?

More detailed questioning as to prospects, training availability, remuneration, expenses and assistance with relocation will depend upon the level of interest shown in you by the interviewer.

Nevertheless, before walking away you should be certain as to these aspects, along with contract details if appropriate, in case you are offered the post. They may change their mind if you ask for another interview to find these things out!

Certainly you should know what salary is offered, along with details of 'perks', if any, and pension arrangements. Negotiating a salary is fraught with danger but, if you refer back to your basic criteria, you will have a figure up your sleeve if the recruiter insists on your quoting one. A way round this, if you prefer, is to say what you earned in your most recent position and turn the question around by asking 'What did you have in mind?'

If the question of salary comes up very early in the interview, unless a specific figure is mentioned it is probably better for you to suggest that you would like to hear more about the job content before deciding upon its value. Most interviewers will respect this view and allow the discussion to continue without reference, until later, to levels of remuneration.

If it becomes clear that the job for which you are applying is going to pay something far less than your 'reserve', do not be put off too early but hope that you can convince your questioner that you are worth more. Very few jobs today carry hard and fast salaries; most are related to a scale which may be quite wide and, if it is felt that you are the man for the job, you may well qualify for the higher figure immediately.

Job interviews are rarely conclusive and you will probably be left with the message: 'We will let you know.' Always assume the worst and that way you will not be disappointed; certainly do not stop your job search merely because your hopes have been raised during one interview. Others to be seen after you may impress even more!

You may be called to a further interview, but do not assume yet that you have the job. For more important positions, it is quite common for employers to see prospective employees more than once and sometimes by different interviewers. This is where your earlier answers may be cross-checked and, for this reason if none other, ensure consistency in what you say.

Psychological Tests

These are becoming more commonplace, especially for top jobs. The art of graphology, although still in use, has been overtaken by the psychologist, with some of the larger firms employing their own.

If you are faced with a test of this nature, do not try and beat the system; it is impossible. Treat it very seriously and provide straightforward, honest answers, not those you believe are being sought. Questions have been designed with infinite care and whilst they may appear in random order, your reactions are tested against well-documented data guaranteed to throw up any traits either for or against you. Employers using these methods are beginning to have great faith in them and you are advised not to attempt any 'cheating'.

These tests normally take the form of a series of questions to which you are expected to respond in a set time. Do not worry yourself if you do not complete the test; it is intended that time should be against you and, unless you are superhuman, there will probably be a few unanswered questions at the end. These are often 'duplicates' of questions asked earlier in the test and ignored by the tester. Do not linger too long over any one question. Pace yourself as far as possible to achieve something like 80 per cent of the answers; if one stumps you completely, move on immediately and, if there is time, come back to it at the end.

You are probably being tested in a series of areas, although this may not be evident at the time. These may include:

- Your personality type;
- Likes and dislikes;
- Numeric and logistical ability;
- General intelligence;
- Decision-making; and
- Aptitude for the job.

Another type of test you may meet is the behavioural exercise, normally held within small groups. A task will be set which has to be completed within a known time-scale and you will be allocated a role, such as 'Officer Commanding' or 'Transport Manager', which may bear no relation at all to the job for which you have applied. Commonsense is all that is called for, although this type of exercise can be somewhat daunting at first sight and, for the employer, not always easy to assess candidates' aptitudes.

If you do find yourself in a group situation, try to follow a line somewhere in the middle where you neither dominate nor shirk from playing a part. Remain positive and keep a careful note of what is happening as it occurs; if there is time for note-taking, this could prove invaluable if you are called upon for a summary.

It is almost impossible — and there is rarely time — to guess what the assessors are seeking, so do not even try. Do your best, maintain confidence and you will be in with a chance.

Seeing the Middleman

An increasing number of employers are using middlemen, or consultants, to provide them with a short-list of suitable candidates and, whilst your interview technique and etiquette will not differ, you may have to operate 'in the dark'. It is quite feasible, for instance, that you will not know the prospective employer's name nor even his location, for you will have responded to a job advertisement quoting a description and little else.

It is the consultant's task to screen candidates and to save much of his principal's time by weeding out those unlikely to fit the bill.

The interview is likely to be general rather than specific, at least at first, until you have aroused sufficient enthusiasm for the consultant to find out a little more about you. At the early stage he is likely to ask you questions about your life-style, general experience and aspirations. If these do not equate with his master's known needs, he will probably let you know without further ado.

If, however, he believes that you have the right blend of experience and style, he will question you further to make quite certain that you are likely to 'fit' into the organisation which has commissioned him. More and more employers are looking for 'right fits' as much as they are seeking more basic qualities and it is the consultant's job to make the jigsaw work. For this reason, he may delve quite deeply into your personal life and this you must expect. He also wants to be certain that this is the right career move for you and that you are likely to stay; if, after a while, your placement does not work out, he is unlikely to see his next fee!

As the interview develops, seek answers to your own questions as well as responding to points raised, for this will also help the consultant in assessing whether to recommend that your name goes forward.

Facing a Panel

Some government institutions prefer this method, where you can face anything up to five or six people at the same time.

Daunting as this might appear, it calls only for an increased degree of confidence on your part resulting, hopefully, in a more relaxed atmosphere in which you can feel at home as questions come hurtling at you.

There will normally be a chairman who may or may not introduce his colleagues. He will kick off the questioning and then either ask another panel member to take over or there will be general questioning from every quarter!

Smile as much as is appropriate and try to look, however briefly, at each member of the panel as you provide each answer, no matter where the source. This way they will all feel involved and have a greater affinity with you than if you look directly only at your questioner.

Pause, if necessary, before answering difficult questions and never forget that you would not have been asked if they had not been interested in you; something must have been in your favour!

The Post Mortem

As soon as possible after each interview make brief notes of good and bad points and, in general, what you thought of it. These may prove invaluable at a later date and, if you are having a tough run, go over them with a close friend or relation to judge where you might be going wrong.

Being interviewed is a technique and one that not many of us receive much practice in, so do not be too downhearted in the early days if success is eluding you. You are probably getting better at it all the time, especially if you are prepared to dissect each interview and discuss it with someone you can trust.

Your day will come!

CHAPTER 10

Working Abroad

One way in which many people have found themselves a better job is by looking overseas. In the post-war years, boatloads made their way to Australia to seek fame and fortune; many found both.

But that was in darker days, when job opportunities were more limited than they are today and before our basic industries had found time to pick themselves up again after the war. Now, generally, there are equal opportunities wherever you look; the job market has become a global one.

You will, therefore, be competing with Germans, Americans, Italians and so on, in fact any nationality which has learned to train its workers in a skill that is internationally recognised. People such as doctors, nurses, teachers, engineers, chefs and accountants — language permitting — are able to offer their skills to the highest bidder in any country. And a spell abroad can look impressive on a c.v.

Fortunately, whilst you will always be in competition, the British expatriate is still regarded very highly abroad and, because our training is invariably more intense and deep-seated, this means that you can quite often command higher salary levels and more attractive perquisites.

Working for a British or multi-national company abroad, as opposed to working for a local concern, also has its advantages in terms of security, living conditions and trips back home. In this type of case, contracts are usually for periods of between one and three years and you therefore have a planned 'exit route' after your spell abroad, although finding the next job is not too easy from many thousands of miles away!

If yours is an internationally recognised skill, and your family circumstances are such that a British base is not essential, at least for a time, then do cast your eye over the foreign job market. That better job may well be sitting waiting for you in Azerbaijan!

Although the oil boom has been and gone, there still remain many developing countries desperate for 'teachers' in every discipline to communicate knowledge to their own nationals before they are in a position to take over. In the medical, educational and technological spheres, for instance, numerous vacancies still await the right British applicant and it should not be an area for you to ignore if this is your field.

Teachers of English, of course, are always wanted and teaching your native tongue as a foreign language can be very rewarding. Royal Society of Arts 'English as a Foreign Language' courses are available, either during the evenings or by way of a four or eight week stint; the RSA Diploma may alternatively be taken via a correspondence college.

Europe beyond 1992 offers boundless opportunities and now is the time to start planning for these.

Working abroad is one thing; living there is an entirely different matter. Changes in culture, eating habits, religion, education and so many other aspects of day to day life have to be absorbed and accepted; to ignore them — or, worse, fly in the face of them — will prove fatal and all your best efforts will be wasted. Going abroad, therefore, has to be tackled in a sensible manner and, once again, your knapsack baton is going to come in very handy!

The Public Sector

Thousands of Britons have found working abroad for a spell very satisfying in the public sector. They are well cared for, have their educational and other needs especially catered for where they are grouped in larger numbers and have a sense of belonging to an established community. India is a good example of having 'schooled' hundreds of families from the United Kingdom earlier this century before that country went its own way.

Our Government's Ministry of Overseas Administration looks after a whole population of employees serving in foreign countries. Advisers, under the guise of Technical Co-operation Officers, are sent in particular to developing countries and normally paid at UK rates along with an inducement allowance and a further addition related to the cost of living overseas. Air, or sometimes boat fares are paid both ways and help is given in other ways to smooth the initial passage of a family moving abroad to work for the first time.

The Armed Forces, of course, expect to carry out an overseas spell of duty, whilst the Diplomatic Service and the Crown Agents also have many of their employees working abroad at any one time.

Two schemes of co-operation exist between the British Government and those overseas under the wing of either the Overseas Service Aid Scheme or the British Expatriates Supplementation Scheme. The Overseas Development Administration also operates the Technical and Training Organisation for Overseas Countries, supplying professional advisors in the areas of agricultural education, industrial training, public administration and the development of management.

There are also the international institutions such as the European Commission, the International Monetary Fund, the World Bank, the Red Cross and the United Nations. All seek skilled employees to fill vital posts abroad, normally for short contractual periods.

Where to Start Looking

Before you begin to look anywhere, consider your present employer. If he has sites abroad, or even operates through agents or representatives in foreign lands, consider an approach to discuss what opportunities might lie in that direction. If a large group, does it have an overseas parent, subsidiary or associate?

Do not go in with a blank expression, though. Do your homework thoroughly and sift ideas and possibilities in your mind before putting a positive suggestion to your employer; he will then take it more seriously than if you merely enquire what overseas opportunities there might exist in his organisation.

Failing that, it is back to the Press, in the main. UK national newspapers remain one of the best sources for jobs abroad, coupled with searches of appropriate trade journals and professional magazines. Probably the most fertile ground lies in the quality Sunday newspapers.

Obtain regular copies of *Executive Post*, published by the overseas division of the Professional and Executive Recruitment organisation. For graduates, there are *Graduate Post*, *Graduate Opportunities* and annual career directories, although the latter should be used as general guidance only.

Of course, recruitment agencies, search consultants and similar professional associations will be ready to act for you here and reference should be made back to Chapter 6.

You may also see advertised newsletters available for those interested in overseas vacancies, but beware unless they come from a reputable, and preferably known, source, for it is often a case of 'It's your money they're after' and hefty upfront consultation fees can come to naught.

Two other possibly fruitful sources should be considered. One is to read regularly a good newspaper for items referring to UK companies branching out overseas where you should not be afraid to make a direct approach (with your c.v.) before advertisements begin to appear. Your pioneering spirit may be rewarded!

The other is to write 'on spec' letters to foreign based companies, again sending your c.v., expressing interest in specific vacancies which might arise. It is perfectly acceptable for your letter to be written in English, although clearly if you are fluent in the local language, then take advantage of this. Research, though, must be just as thorough as if you were following this line at home and here your local library will probably be able to assist to seek out details of the company of your choice.

Family Considerations

If you are part of a family unit, then normally the rest of the gang need to be behind you. Do not badger them into agreeing with you; consider each of their needs, look carefully into how these will be met and then hold a family council. Whatever the age of any of your family, your moving abroad will have an impact upon them. Babies can be susceptible to foreign illnesses and diseases; school children will obviously need to adapt (which, generally, they do quite remarkably); and spouses will clearly have to learn to live in a different environment.

Educational needs are probably the most difficult area to make decisions upon before you depart. Even leaving children behind in boarding schools poses its own problems; what happens, for instance, during holiday periods?

Enquire what educational facilities are available in the country of your choice. Does the company have its own school, or can it make local arrangements on your behalf? Is there a school especially for expatriates' children in the locality? Could home teaching be considered?

Although employers tend to help with educational costs, their level of assistance may not necessarily fully meet your total outlay and this will need clarifying at the outset.

Very young children — under five — will find few facilities to meet their special needs abroad, for we educate our children in the UK from a younger age than most other countries. Local expatriate wives do, however, pull together to organise their own playschool groups and children fresh from Britain quickly become accustomed to often slightly different surroundings but basically a similar environment. Several organisations exist offering specialist help, in particular the Worldwide Education Service, part of the Parents' National Educational Union, which provides a comprehensive nursery package.

Many overseas schools operating in the English language are based upon American teaching methods, due merely to the large number of Americans operating abroad. Children up to the age of about 10 should cope adequately with the differences, but above that age you should give consideration to preparing them for the British examination system.

It becomes more difficult to find suitable education abroad for older children, for many secondary pupils of expatriate parents tend to find themselves left in boarding schools over here. Most, it must be said, enjoy the sometimes spoiled existence but every child is different and its emotional needs must be slotted into your priority considerations before accepting a post overseas. Help can be obtained from the Independent Schools Information Service.

If there appears no alternative to having your children taught at home, again the Worldwide Education Service can assist with providing the sources of teaching materials and providing guidance and other advice. Teaching packs are available suitable for all ability levels up to GCSE standard.

The Service is a registered charity with long experience of teaching methods for expatriates' offspring. Teaching is under their guidance via a 'home school service' and regular assessments are made through a tutor to whom you report at set intervals; when visiting the UK, you are encouraged to visit the tutor at the same time with your child.

Distance learning courses are also available from several private colleges but, as with the WES scheme, a great deal of parental input is essential to guarantee success and you or your partner will have to allocate the necessary time as instructed in the course material.

Along with educational considerations go health aspects and clearly all the necessary inoculations and vaccinations require attending to. Larger employers invariably make the arrangements for you but independently sought advice is recommended to ensure that every necessary precaution is taken. Several weeks may be needed for 'jab' results and up-front planning is thus essential.

You may also care to consider taking with you a spare pair of spectacles, contact lenses or even false teeth! Obtaining new ones in foreign parts can often test the patience of a saint!

The Money Side

Salary levels abroad at first sight bring a glint into most executives' eyes but until a true comparison with local living costs has been carried out, do not get carried away.

A remuneration package is usually offered comprising much more than basic salary, but do determine before commitment precisely what it contains; a full check-list appears below. Accommodation assistance is probably the most important item calling for definition, but ask also about electricity and water bills, educational and insurance costs, whether a company car is included and, certainly in the less developed areas, whether staffing assistance is paid for.

Pension rights should be established, as well as family benefits should the worst arise. Check also your holiday entitlement and what assistance, if any, is provided for visits back to the UK. Do these include all of your family?

You will obviously wish to know in what currency you are to be paid and, equally importantly, whether some of the funds may be transmitted back to the UK. Experienced expatriates will also know that salaries can, under certain circumstances, be directed towards a third country tax haven!

Above all, find out about local living costs. The management consultancy, PE Inbucon, regularly reports on these around the world and some of their findings are quite revealing. The list below gives a very rough indication of comparisons with London but use it as a guide only, for variations will occur, as they do everywhere, and exchange rate movements will also distort the figures. £100 worth of living costs in London will cost you the following in other major cities:

London	£100
Tokyo	£164
Bucharest	£131
Oslo	£128
Zurich	£123
Stockholm	£117
Vienna	£107
Moscow	£105
Paris	£104
Milan	£102
Brussels	£102
Berlin	£100
Madrid	£ 97
Los Angeles	£ 92
New York	£ 91
Singapore	£ 86
Sydney	£ 84
Nicosia	£ 82
Lisbon	£ 80
Bangkok	£ 74
Kingston	£ 70
New Delhi	£ 66

Taxation, of course, is another story and you would be well advised to seek independent advice from, say, one of the major accountancy firms, all of whom have people on board especially there to help you.

Residency, for normal purposes, must be defined, as must your domicile — and do not imagine these mean the same to the tax inspector! You may also need to establish your continuing right to MIRAS, or Mortgage Interest Relief at Source.

National Insurance considerations will differ whilst you are living abroad and in order to continue your right to benefits, you must consider making voluntary contributions.

Not many other countries have anything to rival our own National Health Service, and private medical insurance thus really comes into its own.

There exist two useful schemes to avoid paying VAT: one relating to motor cars and one to other items. VAT forms 411 and 408 respectively apply and your local office will give you all possible assistance. In each case you must reside abroad for at least one full year , but do not rush out and buy that car before taking advice, for certain procedures must be followed.

Finally, before signing on the dotted line take legal advice on your contract. Any good employer will not be at all surprised and, indeed, if he is, then that alone is sufficient reason for your doing so.

You should know, for instance, under what legal system your contract is written and what your legal redress might be in the case of a dispute. A full job specification might be included and this will prove a suitable opportunity to give this a detailed examination. The contract may even be in a foreign language and a full English translation should be called for. If your contractual period is a set one, find out before you sign what rules and regulations apply in the case of renewal.

Where Should You Look?

The world may be your oyster but it will be as well to cast about to ensure you find the pearl.

Foreign countries, quite naturally, vary enormously in climate, living conditions, infrastructure, and so many other important facets of everyday living that the same job in, say, Africa may not be as appealing as in central Europe. You must not get carried away, therefore, by the job itself; it is equally important to look at its precise location and be as satisfied as you can be, after diligent research, that you are going to be happy living there.

Take a close look at the sort of things that are going to affect you on a daily basis, such as:

- How will you travel to work?
- What sort of social life will be available for you and your family?
- What types of foodstuffs are on sale in the shops?
- How far will you be living from centres of civilization?
- Is the climate likely to suit you?
- How will any children fare in strange surroundings?

The answers you provide will be very different in a place like America than in, say, India. If you are hesitant in a number of areas, then that country is probably not for you. Age tends to be a limiting factor here, for the older we become the more set in our ways we become; countries still developing are more likely to suit the young than the old. If home comforts really mean something to you, do not be attracted falsely by wide open spaces thousands of miles away.

Legal formalities can bar the entry of foreigners to many overseas spots and it can take, for instance, up to two years to establish permanent relocation in America. Permits are invariably required whilst certain countries debar the entry of some foreign nationals.

Mainland Europe itself can be a disappointment. Hundreds of Britons have attempted to work happily over there, only to return somewhat frustrated after a few months. Pay is not always what it appears to be and apparently solid contracts melt overnight; legal advice is essential.

The Middle East has traditionally taken a lot of workers from the UK, although lower oil prices have resulted in cut-backs and some firms which established offices there have since pulled back. Europeans, too, can find the stringent Islamic laws forbidding, where cases involving alcohol can lead to instant deportation — or worse. Wearing a bikini will certainly attract police attention, even in the privacy of your own garden, and unless you are willing to adopt a strict 'whilst in Rome' approach, then you will be safer at home.

Local business etiquette, wherever you are, must be followed, in the same way that you would at home. Good manners are universal, but it is important that you learn in what category various practices fall in the country of your choice.

Women in some overseas countries will not have the freedom which they enjoy here. In Saudi Arabia, for instance, women are generally not allowed to work nor to drive and often have to be accompanied when they leave the house.

As long as Hong Kong is a British colony, opportunities there remain good, as they do throughout the Far East although some are beginning to tighten up on immigration regulations.

Africa has always welcomed British workers and thousands have found the way of life there very much to their liking. Personal security can, however, be a worrying problem in certain parts and remuneration overall remains modest.

Your best opportunity to work abroad will be gained if you are able to speak the language of the country and this will become increasingly important throughout Europe as we approach 1992. Most mainland Europeans have already stolen a march on us, learning English from a young age, and we have a lot of catching up to do if we are to compete seriously in the newly created job market.

French is a must for the Common Market, whilst in Spain and Latin America, Spanish is essential. The more 'exotic' languages, such as Japanese and Russian, will put you well ahead of the field if you are fluent in any one of these.

Language colleges are based in all major towns and although an inordinate amount of time must be devoted to learning a new language from scratch, it will be well worth while if you are to be a serious competitor in the international job market.

Planning Your Finances

A carefully chosen financial advisor, used wisely before you become too committed, will be worth his weight in gold. For a start, you will probably have more money to spare than formerly, it may be paid in a foreign currency, local taxation will certainly differ from the UK, and you will want to ensure a safe financial base for when you eventually return home. There are enough reasons there alone not to attempt financial planning in a foreign country on your own.

Some of the major UK banks offer expatriate services, whilst membership of FIMBRA (Financial Intermediaries, Managers and Brokers Regulatory Association) should pin-point an experienced financial advisor, although not necessarily one specialising in expatriates' needs and this is what you should seek out.

Banking arrangements need consideration, with the emphasis upon safety of your hard-earned funds. If you can select a correspondent bank linked to your UK based one, the transfer of funds between the two will become easier and any problems should more quickly become resolved. Remember that cashpoint machines are not always as readily available abroad as they are here and special arrangements may have to be put in place to ensure the regularity of liquid funds.

Taxation will inevitably have an impact upon where you base your banking facilities and, here again, specialised advice is imperative.

What to do about a home owned in the UK is another sticky subject, for problems can abound with letting tenants in and yet, if you decide to sell, you may well find house prices have leapt during your spell abroad when you return. No one can really answer this testing question for you, although good advice can always be listened to. If you are uncertain, however, it is probably best to sell and make a fresh start at a later date; at least this way you will not find yourself in the unenviable position of having to go to court to discharge tenants unwilling to leave, which has occurred more than once.

A Final Checklist

We have only here highlighted a few of the more obvious potential pitfalls (and opportunities) of working abroad. It is recommended that you study the subject more seriously if this alternative is one which attracts and, in particular, *Working Abroad: The Daily Telegraph Guide to Working and Living Overseas* will help to put you right.

The following employment conditions check-list (abbreviated where necessary) is taken from that publication (extracts with permission from *Working Abroad: The Daily Telegraph Guide to Working and Living Overseas*, 11th edition, Golzen, G., 1988, published by Kogan Page, London):

1. Is your employer going to meet the cost of travel out from the UK for your family as well as yourself?

2. Is he going to provide accommodation?

3. If accommodation is free, but there is a subsidy, how is this assessed?

4. Who is going to pay for utilities?

5. If there is no subsidy and accommodation is not free, are you sure your salary is adequate?

6. Will the employer subsidise or pay for your and your family's hotel bills for a reasonable period until you find somewhere to live? Is the figure realistic?

7. Will you be paid a disturbance allowance?

8. What arrangements will be made to cover legal and other fees if you have to sell your UK home or any difference if you have to let your home between the rental income and outgoings?

9. Will you be paid a clothing allowance?

10. Will your employer pay for or subsidise household items that you will need in a hot climate?

11. Will your employer provide/subsidise the cost of domestic servants?

12. Is a car going to be provided with the job — with or without a driver?

13. Will the employer pay for or subsidise club membership and/or entrance fees?

14. Will you be paid an allowance for entertaining?

15. If your children attend UK boarding schools, what arrangements are there for them to join you in the holidays?

16. What arrangements are there for your own leave?

17. Will the employer pay for/subsidise all or any additional insurance premiums you may incur?

18. If social security payments are higher than in the UK, will your employer make up the difference?

19. Will he contribute to your medical expenses if free medical attention is not available or inadequate?

20. If your salary is expressed in sterling would you be protected against loss of local buying power in case of devaluation? Equally, if your salary is in local currency, would it be adjusted for a rise in sterling against that currency?

21. Is your salary in any way index-linked to the cost of living?

22. If there are any restrictions on remittances, is your employer prepared to pay a proportion of your salary into a UK bank or that of some other country with a freely negotiable currency?

23. Does your employer contribute towards language teaching for you and/or your spouse?

24. Is the legal status of your appointment clear?

25. Have all the terms of the job and provisions of the remuneration package been confirmed in writing?

26. Are the contract and conditions of employment subject to English law and, if not, do you or your advisors clearly understand how they should be interpreted should a dispute arise?

27. If the job is with a foreign company, there are a number of points that need special attention:
    (a) Are the duties of the job clearly spelled out in writing in a contract of employment?
    (b) Are the normal working hours laid down? How long will your journey to work be?
    (c) Are all matters affecting pay clear and in writing?
    (d) If there is a bonus, are the conditions under which it is due unambiguous?
    (e) Are there satisfactory arrangements for sick pay?
    (f) Would there be any restriction on your changing jobs if you got a better offer from another employer or decided to leave?
    (g) Do leave conditions clearly specify whether the leave is home or local?
    (h) Will legitimate expenses be paid in addition to salary?
    (i) Have you taken any steps to check the bona fides of the prospective employer?

This comprehensive list alone provides a clear guide to the necessary depth of your researches and enquiries before you sign anything; ignore it at your peril!

CHAPTER 11

Working for Yourself

Being your own boss may or may not have occurred to you as an alternative to your present occupation. If not, it is certainly worthy of consideration.

We can only, in one brief chapter, take a look at what aspects you should weigh up before either discarding this alternative, or perhaps taking it one step further. If you believe you should dig deeper, then further study is essential and you may care to read *How to Start and Run Your Own Business*, by the same author as this book, (see Further Reading) from which much of the following is taken.

Weighing Up Your Present Situation

Sit down and take a cold, statistical look at yourself, your job and your environment. Break these down and take stock of all the many benefits which you may currently enjoy and which, in your search for pastures new, you may be overlooking.

Your major asset will almost undoubtedly be job security, although this will naturally be very dependent upon your occupation. If you are unfortunate enough to be unemployed, then the security factor becomes irrelevant.

Do you work set hours, or, considered another way, are you fairly certain at what time your next meal will be? This is just one of a number of 'assets' which you may have to forego if you intend to take the path of self-employment. Let us look at some of the others.

Does your job attract 'perks', such as a company car, luncheon vouchers, cheap travel or goods, or even just a subsidised canteen? These are all worth hard cash and, if working for yourself, will have to come out of profits, your new form of income.

What about pension rights? Leaving a pensionable post can be an expensive exercise, although the law is now a little fairer on this point than it was in the past.

To what degree of stress are you subjected? This will without doubt increase dramatically if you work for yourself.

Perhaps you have some degree of responsibility which you relish; we will assume that you want a lot more!

Your statutory rights are important and cannot be ignored in today's legislative society. Laws do, however, tend to be in the employee's favour and you will thus become subject to them instead of being protected by them if you 'change sides' and become an employer. Certainly if you have a trade union behind you, this can prove a powerful ally in times of dispute, sickness or accident. If you become a 'boss', it may become a force with which you will have to contend.

Finally, still looking at the favourable aspects of employment, have you overlooked companionship and, possibly, congenial working conditions? Both could disappear, at least initially, if you become a 'one-man band', working in less favourable conditions.

Making Comparisons

So far the comparisons have been general rather than specific and you will obviously be more interested in your own special case. Go about this in the following way: list, under a series of headings, what you feel you have now and what you believe to be the case if you were working for yourself. Here is an example, comparing a factory worker with a retailer:

Employee	Retailer
Geographical Area: Industrial	Perhaps of your choice?
Immediate Place of Work: Factory	Shop
Hours Worked: Say 8 a.m. to 4 p.m. five days a week. Some overtime?	60/70 hours per week very likely. Certainly Saturdays and perhaps Sunday mornings. Unsocial hours.
Holidays 4 weeks annually plus Bank Holidays?	Probably none in the first few years unless a relative stands in. Bank Holidays will have to be worked in certain trades.
Working atmosphere: Noisy, smelly, stuffy?	Should be clean and airy. But do not forget that some of the backroom jobs may be less pleasant, e.g. cutting up bacon.
Type of Work: Monotonous?	Varied but certainly busy at times, boring at others.
Companionship Probably very good.	You may be on your own for a lot of the time, although customers will be there to talk to.

Employee	Retailer
Responsibility:	
Perhaps very little?	Absolute!
Administration/Organisation:	
Dependent upon responsibility.	Again, very full. Bookkeeping, VAT, PAYE, etc.
Daily Travel:	
Car or public transport? Time 'wasted' — perhaps 30 to 60 minutes daily?	If you are living over the shop, no problems here.
Leisure/Lifestyle:	
Evenings and weekends free at the present to follow social life? Enough surplus earnings to save for occasional luxuries?	Restricted, perhaps, to Sundays and half a day weekly. Remember that stock purchases have to be organised, books made up. Profits may need to be ploughed back in the early years. Some leisure pursuits will have to be abandoned.
Prospects:	
Limited? Further qualifications needed for promotion? 'Dead men's shoes' syndrome?	Can be unlimited and subject to personal capabilities and financial resources only.

You will see, incidentally, that financial considerations feature only lightly in this assessment; what you are trying to do at this stage is to check out whether self-employment is for YOU.

So What About You?

How are you going to know whether you are a member of that exclusive club of people who possess the rare qualities, many of them entirely instinctive, needed to make a success of going it alone?

This is where you must, once again, analyse the real YOU. No psychiatrist's couch is needed, just an unlimited degree of unadulterated honesty on your part.

Imagine you are ready to meet your maker and only perfectly honest answers to the following third-degree questionnaire are going to guarantee the issue of the passport you need to get through the pearly gates, except in this case you want those marked 'Self Employed This Way':

Temperament

What kind of attitude do you possess? Are you easy-going, prepared to accept the status quo, and somewhat annoyed when changes cloud the horizon? Or are you eager for new challenges, ready to adapt, and accept improvements?

Leadership

Have you a preference for taking orders, or giving them? Do you find it frustrating to have to accept instructions from others when you feel that, left alone, efficiency would result if your own ideas were followed?

Do you feel competent in dealing with subordinates, or does every awkward instruction create tension in your breast?

Could you competently deal with unsavoury decision-making such as the giving of notice to a colleague? Or would such thoughts be undermined by allowing your heart to overrule your head?

Willpower

If a goal has been set, have you sufficient willpower to strike at achievement without waiving? To set your course and not allow minor crises to upset you?

Past personal experiences should come to mind, pin-pointing your success, or otherwise, in reaching previously set goals.

'Stickability' sums up the necessary attribute here and, granting some adaptability, you should know whether you can honestly tick the 'Yes' or 'No' column.

Confidence

This is essential. Without it, some of the other factors will lack the strength of character you seek in order to succeed. Do you have confidence in your own ability and does this confidence come over when dealing with others, whether subordinates, peers or customers?

We all tend to sum up a newcomer in the first 30 seconds of speaking to him and it is within that vital fraction of time that you must 'sell' yourself.

Security

Are you a believer in personal and family protection, in the form of a secure salaried position, or are you ready to face insecurity in the hope that its rewards, mentally and financially, will in time be to your advantage?

This risk factor is, probably, the greatest one and for a family man or woman, there are considerations beyond care for one's own skin.

Health

Working for yourself produces great demands on both mental and physical resources. Can you withstand such pressures? Stress will undoubtedly increase and there will be little time for sick leave!

Family Aspects

Husbands, wives and children all feature in the plan you have in mind; have you carefully considered each one? Schooling, holidays or a change of home, as we have suggested earlier, may all prove upsetting, and the psychological as well as the practical angles should be analysed, preferably in a 'family council'.

Expertise

Most human beings are particularly good at something and both natural as well as technical abilities should be listed. Attributes in manual, intellectual and organisational fields call for investigation as well as a close look at your own hobbies and interests. These can invariably provide clues as to the type of individual you are.

If you have no practical experience of the field you hope to enter, you may well be wasting your time. No amount of enthusiasm can cover up a complete lack of knowledge.

Dozens of bodies exist ready to train you and some of these have been looked at in Chapter 5; take another look at them now to identify those which can assist your going it alone.

Taking Advice

Above all, research. And then research some more. Let that be your motto.

One of the best ways of adding to your increasing store of knowledge is to talk over your ideas with other people. Two heads are always better than one and the more heads you take advantage of the better. Speak to friends, relatives and neighbours. Bounce ideas off them. You will be surprised how rewarding this exercise can be and just how keen others are to put you on the right track. Remember, though, to listen; let them do the talking. Afterwards, sift their ideas and make your own decisions!

Your bank manager can be the ideal springboard to begin your bouncing. He will normally be quite prepared to chat in general terms at an early stage although make clear to him that you are merely formulating ideas prior to the possibility of returning to him with a formal business plan. He will usually have seen it all before and his comments and ideas will, therefore, be based upon practical experience.

Talk, also, to people in the trade in which you are interested. You need not tell them your specific ideas, for clearly they may become competitors, but weigh up what they tell you with your own researches before making up your mind.

If you have retailing in mind, write to the National Union of Small Shopkeepers of Great Britain and Northern Ireland who have over 10,000 members and who will provide helpful advice.

Similarly, most occupations liaise through a trade body and proper enquiries should soon reveal the source you require. The Small Firms Service is a Government sponsored organisation set up to advise both new and established businesses through several offices in England, Scotland and Wales. A series of first-class brochures ranging in titles from 'A Big Help to a Small Business' through 'Obtaining a Franchise' to 'Starting a Manufacturing Business' are obtainable free of charge from the centres.

Chambers of Trade and Commerce are also willing to assist, although they tend to deal with already established businesses in the main.

A good solicitor and accountant will be ready to offer suitable professional advice, although not normally without cost.

Investigating the Market

If you have by now reached the stage where you would like to investigate further a particular product or service, then conduct as full a market survey as you are able, given cost and time constraints, before going further.

How wide an appeal, for instance, will your idea have? Is it something — such as Blackpool rock — that will have a limited geographical market, or is the potential on a national, or even international, scale?

What is the current consumption level? Is it, like bread, widely bought or, like silver presentation tankards, a now and again item?

Is it cheap or expensive? If the latter, then its appeal is going to be limited to the better-off. Thus you may be unwise to set up your stall in an area of high unemployment.

How specialised are you aiming to be? Bicycle clips are sold, although the buying fraternity is a dwindling one.

Is design an important factor? Or packaging? Many manufacturers, aided and abetted by modern department store techniques, have learned how vital it is to catch the public's eye. 'That looks nice' aimed at a packaged cake is merely a compliment to the artist, but it sells the cake.

Is your product a bulky one and thus restricted to the able- bodied, or is it conveniently carried and readily grasped by today's instant shopper?

Take a close look at your intended consumer. Might this person, who is going to pay your wages, be of either sex or is yours a strictly male or female line? If it is either of these, you have immediately cut out about half the population as potential customers!

Look closely at any technological advances in your intended field, as well as the rapidity of these. Progress may quickly overtake you.

Weigh up also the competition. Remember that if you are going to grab a worthwhile share of the market, it will be at their expense. What might their reaction be? A cut-price policy for a period on their part could, for instance, wipe you off the face of the high street.

If you are put off by all these 'uncontrollable' factors, then self-employment might not be for you. But if you are excited by the thought of competition, read on.

Buying an Established Business

This is clearly the quickest way to establish yourself in your own business, although you may have to pay the cost of the previous owner's success in the form of goodwill. Do find out, though, why he wants to sell. His word alone should not be trusted and you will have to make your own subtle enquiries to establish the real reason; one indicator may be what he intends to do afterwards.

Carry out a thorough survey of the business and find out how long it has been on the market. Just like a popular house, a good business generally sells quite quickly.

A seasonal business will call for careful timing in its purchase, for it would be unwise, for instance, to miss the Christmas boom in the toy trade or to start ice-cream manufacture in the winter.

If the business is a limited liability company and you are acquiring the shares, legal advice is essential to discover exactly what liabilities you are taking over.

If you are relying on local trade, make sure you have a wide knowledge of the area. Walk around and get the 'feel' of the community. Is it a declining or growing one? What developments are taking place or planned? A visit to the local authority should provide most of the answers.

At least three years' audited accounts are important to see to provide the trends of turnover and profits. Go through the figures with your accountant or banker and adjust them as necessary. If a manager was previously employed but you intend taking on this role yourself, some alteration to the wages figure may be called for.

You will become responsible for all resources, be they premises or people, so you have a lot of learning on your hands!

Franchise Operations

Franchising has become one of the fastest growth sectors in the world and in the UK. For instance, there are almost 500 different franchise formats with an average number of units per system of 45. Average annual sales per franchise unit are about £270,000.

In return for a sum of money you are given the right to trade under a nationally recognisable name. The franchisor looks after advertising and training, and provides you with his merchandise and, usually, ongoing management advice. You, however, are left to manage.

Famous names using this method include:

Coca Cola	Swinton Insurance
Wimpy	Spud-U-Like
Golden Egg	Kentucky Fried Chicken
Arnold Palmer golf ranges	Dyno-Rod
BSM Driving schools	Computerland
Prontaprint	Holiday Inns
Spar Grocers	Tie Rack
TNT Parcels service	Fast Frame

and many others.

Some franchise operations are obviously better run than others and as careful a study should be made of your intended 'partner' as if you were going it alone. The British Franchise Association, set up in 1977 to foster franchising in the UK, is a useful regulatory body which has over 100 member companies. Its advice is well worth seeking and they will provide you with an information pack for a small price.

A typical franchisee is married with three children, a mortgage and up to £15,000 to invest. The cost of a franchise can vary enormously as the following table shows:

From £10,000 to £100,000:
TNT Parcels Service
Safeclean
Dyno-Rod
Snappy Snaps
Knobs and Knockers
Tie Rack

Over £100,000:
Perfect Pizza
Wimpy

Be prepared to work very long and unsocial hours. Very few franchises, however, fail, partly no doubt due to the franchisor's desire to make the venture mutually successful!

Franchising contracts normally last between 7 and 10 years and you should certainly obtain legal advice as to the clauses they contain.

The rewards can be very high, but do expect to have to put a lot of effort into the business, especially in the early years.

CHAPTER 12

Career Changes for Disabled People

Whilst, as a disabled person, you will already have recognised that career limitations may be present, there is no reason at all why, if you are currently dissatisfied with your job, that you should not aim for a better one.

This chapter does, however, assume that you are already working or have in the past done so, and does not attempt to outline the many ways and means by which disabled people might initially obtain employment. If you have been recently disabled, but have been used to working before your disablement, then this chapter should prove beneficial.

A more comprehensive study will be necessary for those embarking on seeking employment for the first time, and for this purpose reference should be made to the Further Reading list at the end of this book.

For the newly disabled, the first consideration should be the need, or otherwise, to register officially on the Disabled Persons Register. This is quite voluntary and you may prefer to remain 'anonymous' in this respect, although clearly you must disclose any disability which might affect your working ability to a potential new employer.

It is not always necessary to disclose this at the time of completing an application form although it must certainly be brought up at a later interview, whether you are asked to do so or not. Concealing a disability at this stage which might later adversely affect your working could prove to be a breach of contract on your part and will not endear you to your employer. Be prepared, though, to expand upon any particular problem which you have, its background and, hopefully, what little impact it is likely to have on your working ability. Remember that some employers, especially the larger ones, have set themselves targets of numbers of disabled people they wish to employ and you may well be doing them a favour!

Official registration is possible for anyone who is substantially handicapped by injury, disease or congenital deformity which limits their job horizons, based upon their age, experience and qualifications. Only long-term disablement qualifies.

A leaflet on the subject is available from job centres, and advice can be sought from a Disabled Resettlement Officer (specially trained experts, normally based at job centres) or a Specialist Careers Adviser.

Sheltered workshops, discussed later, often reserve places for officially registered disabled, and those in this category are sometimes given preference for Community Programme vacancies.

Points you need to consider before researching for a better job are no different than those discussed earlier for the able-bodied, but a few extra questions remain, such as:

Am I going to be able to obtain the necessary qualifications for this job?

Will my disability limit me to such an extent that I shall constantly feel frustrated?

What opportunities for promotion will be open to me?

Will travelling to work pose a particular problem?

How much additional strain, if any, will there be on my family if I were in such and such a job?

Am I certain I can cope with both my disability and the responsibilities of this job?

If you are satisfied that none of these will pose a threat to you, then go for it! Thousands of disabled people have proved the world wrong and have successfully held down quite responsible positions; there is no reason why you should not be one of them.

Getting into Training

Increasingly, traditional centres of training for able-bodied people cater additionally for those with a handicap, so your first search — if training is going to be necessary — is to seek these out. It is not necessary, therefore, to go over the contents of Chapter 5 again here, but instead we will concentrate upon bespoke facilities which are available to you.

The Open University, especially, goes out of its way to help those with disabilities and even boasts an Office for Students with Disabilities to co-ordinate the availability of special material. There are Induction Courses for you, normally held at the weekends, and if you are unable to attend examinations, special arrangements are made for you to take these at home. Deaf students can ask for transcripts of the programmes which form part of their course and for those with sight difficulties, audio tapes can be provided.

Of particular interest to those with some managerial experience are the Business Studies Distance Learning Schemes operated by the Employment Department Training Agency through the Business and Technical Education Council. Study at home is acceptable, with the help of video and cassette tapes.

If you are able to get away to a college, the Training Agency operates four which have facilities for the disabled at Mansfield, Durham,

Leatherhead and Exeter. You need to apply through your job centre.

There are, of course, several other residential centres especially established to cater for the needs of the disabled and these are usually privately run, often in part on a voluntary basis. The Spastics Society, MENCAP, Dr. Barnardo's, Spina Bifida Association and the Church of England are just a few of the charitable bodies which can put you in touch with a course and a centre suitable for your needs.

If the thought of a full-blown residential college course puts you off, then consider instead one of the many degree courses available on a part-time study basis. This will naturally take you a little longer (although some prove even this wrong!) but do make enquiries at your local polytechnic or write to the National Bureau for Handicapped Students who maintain very full lists of what is available. They will also advise on grants and any other assistance which might be appropriate to you.

Where to Go for Help

Training apart, several bodies exist to guide you in the right direction.

One of the major ones is Opportunities for the Disabled, in which major employers themselves play a vital part in matching their job requirements to people, who despite some disablement, will fulfil their needs. The service is free both to the employer and the potential employee and famous names like Marks and Spencers and Barclays Bank are involved. They have offices in major cities and their London headquarters is available on 01-726-4961; from there they will point you in the right direction.

Job centre staff should be asked about the Professional and Executive Recruitment (PER) which, although not specialising in the demands of the disabled, is very sympathetic when trying to fill vacancies which could be undertaken by someone whose handicap is not relevant to the job description. PER produces a regular news-sheet entitled *Executive Post* listing hundreds of job requirements.

Graduates are especially catered for by the Disabled Graduates Careers Information Service, whose rationale is to concentrate upon the functional aspects of disablement rather than upon the particular medical condition. It thus evaluates and attempts to utilise to the full the existing functional capacity of each of its 'members'.

The service motivates the disabled graduate to highlight his own assets. and their practical application, and to convince the prospective employer of the value of those assets. Again, big names lie behind its sponsorship and these include IBM, Lloyds Bank, Shell, ICI and many others. A data bank is fed with details of disablement, subjects studied, and the methods, aids and adaptations which have enabled them to perform a wide range of different occupations. The Service can be contacted on 0602-484848.

Another organisation which might help is the Association of Disabled Professionals, founded in 1971 with the following aims:

- to improve the education, rehabilitation, training and employment opportunities available to all disabled people;
- to help·them by encouragement and example fully to develop their physical and mental capacities;
- to find and retain employment commensurate with their abilities and qualifications; and
- to improve public knowledge and acceptance of the capabilities, needs and problems of disabled people, particularly in relation to education and employment.

Much of the Association's work involves combatting the inclination of people to associate disability with inability, and, apart from its General Secretary, all officials are themselves disabled. Write to Mrs. Peggy Marchant, The Stables, 73 Pound Road, Banstead, Surrey, SM7 2HU.

These and many other organisations exist up and down the United Kingdom, eager to help you find that better job. Job Clubs for people with special needs are being encouraged and you should make enquiries locally to see if there is one in your area.

Special Schemes

Many examples of what is commonly referred to as sheltered employment abound, and Remploy is perhaps the best known. Set up by the Government following World War II, it employs some 9,000 severely disabled people who produce goods and services totalling over £80 million per annum. It is the largest supplier of clothing to the Armed Forces and, as well as operating as a subcontractor for most of its work, also markets many products now under its own name.

Dozens of different skills are called for in its 95 production centres and many have learned a craft there which they have taken into their next employment. It is thus both a training ground as well as an employment centre.

In addition, the Government has set up some 27 Employment Rehabilitation Centres in the country where you can be referred for assessment and training. Courses can last for several weeks, following which it is hoped that a return to a more normal working environment can be arranged.

Several Community Programmes also exist to allow those who have not worked for some time to reintroduce themselves into career planning; your source again is your local job centre.

Most of the major charitable organisations specialising in one form of disablement or another operate some form of sheltered employment and you should, therefore, track down the one looking after your own special needs.

Being Your Own Boss

Most of Chapter 11 will apply equally to you and, indeed, you are recommended to read also *How to Start and Run Your Own Business* by the same author as this book and published by the same firm.

Your disablement may be no bar to your being of an entrepreneurial nature, but obviously you will have to think very clearly through your handicap to ensure that it does not inhibit success of its own accord.

Help is again readily at hand in the shape of governmental bodies as well as charitable experts. You will be eligible for assistance under the Enterprise Allowance Scheme if you can raise £1,000 and have been unemployed for over two months. Have a word also with the Co-operative Development Agency (01–839–2988) to see if this type of enterprise will suit you.

Training can be arranged via the various agencies mentioned earlier in this book and certainly a course in business studies is recommended before you get too far down the line.

Working at home, either as an employee or on a subcontracted basis, is becoming more common following the success of pilot schemes involving the use of information technology which is especially suitable for the handicapped. If you are a computer buff, make enquiries of the Training Agency who have been evaluating this type of remote working.

Indeed, if you are already a specialist in any subject, or take an exceptional interest in a hobby or pastime, put your research hat on again and see what practical — and remunerative — use this could be put to. Some ideas are:

Writing on your topic for specialist magazines;
Running a databank for devotees;
Operating a mail order business;
Buying and selling specialised articles, or providing a particular service;
Selling by telephone;
Making such goods as pottery, cakes, knitting and so on;
Carrying out research for institutions such as trade unions, religious bodies, federations, etc;
Designing;

and a whole host more.

It is quite possible, therefore, that the better job *you* are seeking could be working for yourself. Do not rush into it, do take advice but, once committed, ensure success by throwing all your energy into it. That way will encourage others to play their part in helping you to come out on top!

Further Reading

Allen, M., and Hodgkinson, R. 1989. *Buying a Business*, 2nd ed., Graham and Trotman, London.

Bramham, J., and Cox, D. 1987. *Job Hunting Made Easy*. Kogan Page, London.

Cambridge Training Associates. 1984. *What Else Can a Secretary Do? Taking Control of Your Career*. Careers and Occasional Information Centre.

Courtis, J. 1988. *Selling Yourself in the Management Market*. Kogan Page, London.

Darnborough, A., and Kinrade, D. 1988. *Directory for Disabled People*, 5th ed. Woodhead-Faulkner/RADAR.

Fader, S., and Kane, B. 1985. *Successfully Ever After: A Woman's Guide to Career Happiness*. Judy Piatkus.

Golzen, G. 1988. *Working Abroad: The Daily Telegraph Guide to Working and Living Overseas*, 11th ed., Kogan Page, London.

Golzen, G., and Plumbley, P. 1988. *Changing Your Job After 35. The Daily Telegraph Guide*, 6th ed., Kogan Page, London.

Harris, M. 1983. *How to Get a Job*, 3rd ed., Institute of Personnel Management.

Knasel, E. 1986. *Your Work in Your Hands*. National Extension College.

Levene, P. 1988. Better Business Series. *How to Start and Run Your Own Shop*, 2nd ed., Graham and Trotman, London.

Major Companies of Europe 1988, volumes I, II and III, 8th ed., Graham and Trotman, London.

Major Energy Companies of Europe 1989, 2nd ed., Graham and Trotman, London.

Miller, R. 1989. *Equal Opportunities: A Career Guide*, 8th ed., Penguin.

Mogano, M. 1989. Better Business Series. *How to Start and Run Your Own Business*, 7th ed., Graham and Trotman, London.

Morphy, L. 1987. *Career Change: New Working Directions*. Hobson.

Pates, A., and Rosenberg, H. 1984. *What Else Can You Do?* Manpower Services Commission.

Thomson, A., and Rosenberg, H. 1987. *A User's Guide to the Manpower Services Commission*, 2nd ed., Kogan Page, London.

Thompson, M. 1986. *Employment for Disabled People*. Kogan Page, London.

Wallis, M. 1987. *Getting There: Jobhunting for Women*. Kogan Page, London.

Young, D. 1983. *Working Abroad: The Expatriate's Guide*. Financial Times.